# Cook

TRADITIONAL IRISH COOKING WITH MODERN TWISTS

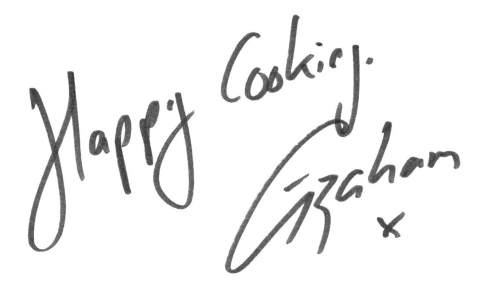

Happy Cooking.
Graham x

Graham Herterich

NINE BEAN ROWS

# Dedication

To Hetch (Dad),

Thanks for all you do and have done for me.

Lots of love, Hetch (Graham)

**Hetch (n.)** Shortened version of Herterich (pronounced Her-ter-itch), this is the nickname given to a member of the Herterich family or the name used to gain the attention of the most senior Herterich in a room. Not to be confused with our pet Shih Tzu, Hetch, who was a special part of our family for 13 years.

# Contents

# Acknowledgements

This book is dedicated to my dad and the life I had growing up at Number 4 Duke Street in Athy, County Kildare. It has become evident to me during the writing of this book that living above our family's pork and bacon butcher shop, and indeed living on Duke Street, has massively influenced the person, chef and baker I am today and for this I will be forever grateful. So to the people of Athy and especially Duke Street, thank you.

Something else has become clear to me during the development of this book, and that is the determination, resilience and resourcefulness of the women of Ireland during the 1980s and 1990s. Don't get me wrong, the women of Ireland have always had these qualities. I'm talking about my own upbringing and experience here. I now look back at that time with very different eyes. Yes, there were tough times, but my overall memories are good, happy ones, and much of that comes down to the work of my mother. So thank you, Mum. I never say it enough.

To all the mammies and daddies, caregivers, guardians and any person who is responsible for the care and wellbeing of young or vulnerable people, thank you.

To Daithí, thank you for all your continued love, support and encouragement.

I would also like to thank the amazing team behind this book, Kristin, Jane, Jo, Orla, Naomi, Ali, Dee and Kate. Thank you all for bringing my life on Duke Street, the food from my childhood and the food I cook now to life.

# Introduction

TRADITIONAL IRISH COOKING IS SUBJECTIVE DEPENDING ON THE PERSON, PLACE AND TIME. FOR ME, THAT WAS LIVING OVER THE FAMILY BUTCHER SHOP AT 4 DUKE STREET IN ATHY, COUNTY KILDARE, WITH MY PARENTS AND FOUR SIBLINGS IN THE 1980S AND EARLY 1990S. WE HAD A PORK BUTCHER SHOP WHERE, ALONG WITH PORK AND BACON, WE SOLD POULTRY, COOKED MEATS AND THE BEST SAUSAGES EVER AND ON FRIDAYS, WE SOLD FISH. THIS BOOK IS HEAVILY INFLUENCED BY MY UPBRINGING AND THAT IS NOWHERE MORE EVIDENT THAN IN THE CHAPTER DEDICATED TO PORK AND BACON.

Two things became apparent to me while I was writing this book. First, I thought that I was simply going to write a list of traditional savoury Irish dishes and pair them with an up-to-date, modern version, like I did in my first book, *Bake*. What transpired, though, was a discovery of the unique ways we eat in Ireland, from the five mealtimes of breakfast, lunch, dinner, tea and supper to particular Irish things such as tea and biscuits, the 'mammy salad' and a Tayto sandwich. But perhaps most importantly, I developed a better understanding of the reasons why we cook and eat the way we do.

I also realised that my thinking about my childhood has shifted. I now look at growing up and living on a main street in a completely different way. For a long time I would have thought that growing up on the street had its downsides. We didn't have a back garden and none of my friends lived close by, things that were important to a young boy. But as I wrote this book, I began to see that Duke Street was one giant playground full of interesting characters, places to explore and people who would have an influence on my life forever.

# Life on Duke Street

Writing about growing up over our butcher shop has also given me time to remember the other shops on Duke Street. Looking back, it won't come as a surprise that the shops I remember most clearly are the food shops or the ones that had a connection to food in some way.
So let's take a little walk up Duke Street.

**Scout Den**

**St John's Lane**

### #21 Coyle's
Home of Ruth and Ernest. Ruth was so talented at embroidery, painting and especially baking. I can still smell her apple tarts. In fact, the apple tart recipe in my first book, *Bake*, was inspired by her.

**Woodstock Street**

**Duke Street**

**William Street**

**Green Alley**

### #24 & 25 Perry's Supermarket
There were three supermarkets in the town and two of them were Perry's. There were no barcodes back then – everything was individually priced with bright stickers.

### #29 Keane's
Keane's was every child's dream. Jars of sweets that were all sold in quarters (as in a quarter pound) filled the shelves: cola cubes that would stick to the brown paper bag in your pocket, satin cushions, sprogs, rhubarb and custard. In my mind there were hundreds of jars, all filled with glorious, multicoloured sugary goodness.

### Maureen Ryan's
Slightly off Duke Street at 6 Lower William Street, Maureen Ryan's was mainly a flower shop but she sold ice cream sandwiches (see page 200) during the summer. Delicious!

## Shaws

Shaws was the department store in the town. I used to love helping at their Christmas party for the local senior citizens, which was held in the shoe department. So many amazing people worked there – Kathleen, Ger, Carmel, Anne, Margaret, Tom and Simon, among others – but I can't think of Shaws without remembering Brendan. He taught me that it was okay to be creative. I will be forever grateful that he was part of my life growing up. He instilled a confidence and self-belief in me that I didn't know I had until later in life.

## McStays

McStays was another butcher shop just across the street from ours. To think that when I was growing up, there were eight butchers in the town: our own shop, D. McStays and Purcell Bros (Duke Street), Pascal Greaney (William Street), Tim Hickey (Emily Square), Hylands Brothers and Barnie Deay (Leinster Street) and Noel Scully (Stanhope Street). Of these, only Hyland Brothers has survived to the present day.

**Duke Street**

## #4 Herterich's

We lived above our pork and bacon butcher shop at Number 4.

## #7 Kevin Watchorn's

A small grocer where us kids would be sent to pick up daily essentials. I still remember buying ½p sweets here.

## #11 Bradbury's Bakery

This is where we'd go for a batch loaf or a soft roll, the sweet smell of sugar filling the air.

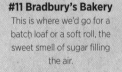

**Convent Lane**

**River Barrow**

## #10 The Gem

A newsagent staffed by Betty, Una, Ber, Rene and May. I used to be fascinated with food magazines. From a young age, I collected the cooking columns that were printed in the back of *Hello* magazine and had a weekly subscription to a recipe magazine that came with its own folders and dividers. I loved going up to the Gem every week to collect it, secretly hoping that Betty would give me a wine gum.

All this is to say that growing up on Duke Street had a massive influence on me from a young age and having all those people around me helped define the person I am today. Even now I will still be reminded of these people and shops at the most unusual times.

# Memories & mealtimes
## in Ireland

When I sat down to write the list of recipes I wanted to include in this book, I hit a blank. Yes, there are classics like bacon and cabbage, Irish stew, porridge, beef and Guinness stew and coddle, all of which are in this book. And yes, there are many more that I could have included, like drisheen and tripe, but those dishes don't represent what was traditional to me in my childhood. So I started writing down ideas based on the mealtimes I had growing up and the food I ate. Very quickly, I had a long list of dishes and foods. It also became clear that the chapters should be based on these traditional mealtimes: breakfast, lunch, dinner, tea and supper.

| Meal | Time | What would you eat? |
|---|---|---|
| **Breakfast** | From sunrise to 12 noon | From something small like a bowl of porridge or tea and toast right up to a full Irish. I am always fascinated by the fact that breakfast is one of the only meals you can have at any time of the day and nobody cares. You could have a bowl of cereal for lunch or a fry for dinner and no one would bat an eye, but if you had lasagne for breakfast, you'd get some funny looks. |
| **Lunch** | 12–3pm | Typically something light, like a bowl of soup or a sandwich. You would normally have lunch if you were having dinner later. |
| **Dinner** | 12–7pm | Dinner is the largest meal of the day. It would be common for some people, especially farmers, to have dinner earlier in the day, but nowadays most people have dinner in the evening. |
| **Tea** | 4–7pm | If you have dinner early, you have tea later in the evening. Tea is a bit like lunch in that it's a light meal but the food at teatime tends to be hot. |
| **Supper** | 6–10pm | Supper can be slightly interchangeable with tea, but when I was growing up it was a light snack or something warm on a cold night before bed. |

# 'Traditional Irish cooking isn't defined by what it is but rather by what it does: it nurtures us, it warms us and it makes us who we are.'

I remember lots of things from growing up in the 1980s in Ireland: the first tills with barcode scanners in the shiny new Pettitt's supermarket, summer camps on the Isle of Man with the Scouts and carefree summers in Courtown, County Wexford. I also still clearly remember the food.

I remember rushing home from school for my lunch on 31 October 1986. Why do that date and that lunch stick out so much? Because it was Halloween and we were having colcannon, but more importantly, and in accordance with tradition, it would be studded with coins wrapped in baking parchment. Even more importantly, Mum had studded it with 20p coins, which had only been released the day before. I brought the coins back into school in the afternoon to show my friends.

I can still remember Mum making lasagne for the first time. When served with coleslaw and chips, it's a dish that has become as Irish as bacon and cabbage. I remember being brought for a Chinese meal to celebrate my confirmation. I remember new foods and spices hitting the shelves of supermarkets – little did I know the impact these modern influences were going to have on my life.

What I don't remember is the recession in the early 1980s. I don't remember how much people struggled to put food on the table. I don't remember the sacrifices people had to make. Don't get me wrong, I do remember some tough times as I got older and that life wasn't always easy, but as I sit here looking back at my time living on Duke Street between 1977 and 1997, my overall memory is one of happiness.

### What is traditional Irish cooking?

Food had a lot to do with this happiness. You see, this happiness was built on a foundation of being fed, being nourished, being kept warm. As I wrote this book, it became clear to me that traditional Irish cooking is about more than just eating – it's about extracting the maximum amount of nourishment, flavour and warmth out of humble ingredients. Think about a simple bowl of Irish stew with lots of hearty vegetables that would keep you warm for hours, in much the same way that a bowl of porridge at breakfast or soup at lunch would.

It doesn't matter if it's a bowl of coddle or a spice bag, traditional Irish cooking isn't defined by what it is but rather by what it does: it nurtures us, it warms us and it makes us who we are.

# A brief history of Irish cooking

BY ALI DUNWORTH

WE DON'T OFTEN THINK ABOUT IT, BUT THERE IS HISTORY IN EVERY KNOB OF BUTTER, CAKE OF BREAD, HEAD OF CABBAGE OR BOILED HAM. THESE SIMPLE FOODSTUFFS HAVE A RICH PAST. THEY HAVE PROVIDED MUCH MORE THAN JUST NOURISHMENT OVER THE CENTURIES.

Irish food has been woven through our folklore, our customs and our livelihoods. It features in poetry, songs and literature. Our food, our farming, our ingredients and our cooking are as much a part of what has shaped Ireland historically as many of the better-known parts of our past.

Just like any good recipe, it all starts with good ingredients – and we've had plenty. Irish food culture and Irish cooking have always been ingredient-led. Our famous temperate (or let's be honest, wet) climate results in exceptional produce that has always been the backbone of how we eat and cook. We know farming has been part of the Irish DNA for thousands of years thanks to archaeological evidence like the Céide Fields in Mayo, the oldest known Neolithic field system in Europe. Along with these historical references, my favourite glimpse into the food of ancient Ireland is through our storytelling and the many Irish folk tales and legends that feature food, giving us a glimpse into how our ancestors cooked and ate.

Many of us know these stories. Fionn Mac Cumhaill burned his thumb on the flesh of the Salmon of Knowledge while it was roasting and then instinctively sucked his thumb to cool the pain, thereby gaining the great knowledge it imparted to him. Queen Medb, the infamous Warrior Queen of Connacht, waged war over cattle but was killed by a hard piece of cheese thrown from a slingshot. In the famous love story of Deirdre and the Sons of Usna, Deirdre dreams of honey and cream. King Conor always slept by three golden apples. There's a catalogue of tales peppered with accounts of hunting, great feasts and *fulacht fia*, the ancient fire pit field kitchens of the Fianna, the legendary soldiers of the High Kings of Ireland. Successful reigns of kings and queens are reflected in stories of feasting on bounteous produce, including salmon, roasted meats and dairy – ingredients we still eat and treasure today.

What we have been doing with these ingredients and how we have been cooking them is a whole other saga, one greatly influenced by our country's tumultuous history. While many generations may have enjoyed Ireland's green larder, when we start to add colonisation, famine, immigration and poverty to the story, those ingredients become harder to come by. Despite many tragic periods in our history, including land grabbing and exporting some of our best foods (and many people), the Irish are a resilient bunch and have had the buoyancy and strength of character to survive and often even thrive. And these struggles? They are part of the reason why, when it comes to food in Ireland, we cherish nourishment, comfort, generosity and home cooking above all else.

In those hard times, much of the population lived in simple dwellings with one fire to heat the home and cook with. Cooking revolved around those fires, so that meant simple unleavened breads and pots of soups or stews. Meat, when eaten, was baked or boiled. Irish stew, for example, often touted as our national dish, was popular because sheep were kept for their wool and milk, so when the meat eventually made it to the table, it was mutton and therefore needed a long cook.

Vegetable soup (or as Graham calls it, 'hotel soup') has roots reaching back to ancient times and has been a constant in Irish kitchens for generations. It remains a comforting staple. Our adopted national vegetable – the potato, of course – has a prominent history in Ireland and continues to play a significant role in Irish lives and traditional Irish cooking. You'll see in this book that Graham is a proponent of the theory that a side of spuds makes everything better (just don't forget the Saxa white pepper).

Pork has also been a big part of our food history. Wild boar roamed ancient Ireland and might have been cooked over a *fulacht fia*. When the pig was then domesticated, they were one of the only animals kept solely as a source of food, so you'd better believe every piece was utilised. Families would come together to rear, fatten and kill a pig, eating 'everything but the squeal'. This is where our penchant for all things pork stems from. To preserve the meat, pork was salted and cured. Hams, bacon and then sausages were made, processes we still use to make products that are still eaten daily in Ireland. From the breakfast fry-up (page 34) to hazlet (page 98) or a classic Dublin coddle (page 94), these traditional pork dishes have stood the test of time for good reason.

The final ingredient in this brief history is the thing that brings everything together: the women of Ireland. Traditionally, it has been women who have fed the nation. I know Graham will not only not mind me saying that, but that he wholeheartedly agrees. In his first book, *Bake*, he dedicated a page to the women who inspire and inspired him, including family, friends and neighbours. Reading the recipes in *Cook*, there is a similar pattern of influence.

Ireland has lived through some challenging times, but all the while, women cooked. In homes, in cottages and even in the Big Houses, they performed daily miracles, feeding big families and households with very little. Their canny cooking has formed the backbone of Irish cuisine. Our breads, stews and go-to dishes are the recipes that these women relied on because they suited their frugal lives. It wasn't until the 1960s that we started to see a shift in the wider culture around women in society. Changing technology in the home, and changing attitudes outside of it, freed women to start branching out of traditional homemaking roles.

Our traditional home-cooked dishes branched out too. Irish food and cooking were seen through a new lens thanks to a changing world and pioneering women like Myrtle Allen. Often referred to as the matriarch of Irish cuisine, Mrs Allen played a huge part in changing how we think about Irish cooking. She immersed herself in Irish food and cooking from her base in Ballymaloe House in County Cork. Throughout her exceptional career, she elevated Irish ingredients and traditional Irish cooking not only here at home in Ireland, but also on a world stage. Her legacy continues to this day as her passion for Irish food and education around it lives on through her daughter-in-law, Darina Allen, and now Darina's daughter-in-law, Rachel Allen, who continue to fly the flag for Irish food at the venerable Ballymaloe Cookery School.

Looking back at the history of Irish food and cooking with Graham's recipes in mind, I'm more convinced than ever that Irish culinary history has not always been given the respect and attention it deserves. How we eat and cook tells us so much. I've garnered a lot of my understanding from the books of the late Bríd Mahon, an Irish folklorist and writer, and also from Regina Sexton, a brilliant food historian who continues to unearth fascinating insights into Irish culinary history. But one of the best ways to delve into the history of Irish food is, of course, by cooking and eating it. Every recipe, every ingredient, has a storied past.

# The modernisation of Irish cooking

## BY DEE LAFFAN

FOR MANY PEOPLE, THE KITCHEN TABLE IS THE HEART OF THE HOME – THE CENTREPIECE FOR FAMILY MEALS, HOMEWORK, CHATS AND ENTERTAINMENT. YET HOW THE IRISH KITCHEN TABLE HAS EVOLVED, BOTH PHYSICALLY AND FIGURATIVELY, REFLECTS HOW IRELAND AND IRISH FOOD HAVE CHANGED – DRAMATICALLY SO – IN A RELATIVELY SHORT SPACE OF TIME.

It was only few decades ago that we cooked over an open fire in the hearth and family meals were always a sit-down affair around the kitchen table. Now fireplaces are becoming obsolete in many homes and the range (a wood-burning cooker) is a thing of the past. We've gone from boiling broths over an open fire to cooking food in an air fryer.

Modern kitchens even include design features that practically eliminate the need for a kitchen table, such as peninsulas and islands where busy families without the time to sit down and have a meal together can eat their food standing up. Or meals are eaten on our laps on the couch as we simultaneously binge food and the latest Netflix show.

Irish food culture has always been a humble one. We would never feel comfortable aligning ourselves with the cuisine of some of our European neighbours, such as France, Spain and Italy. We have a food culture that's as rich as any, but we have been too humble to say that Ireland's food culture is good. This lack of pride leads some people to ask if an Irish food culture even exists – a question you certainly wouldn't hear our EU neighbours asking themselves about their food cultures.

Thankfully, this is changing as our island gains a growing reputation as a food destination. Our pride in our food producers, our incredible regional artisanal produce and our restaurant scene is palpable. Where our food comes from matters to us.

To delve into some of the influences on our food culture, we can take a whistlestop tour of our history, going back to a time when monasteries were dotted across the island and visiting missionary monks would come here from all over the world, bringing with them their knowledge of different foods and spices. Our history of colonisation has seen the Vikings, Normans and British settle here, altering our food landscape in many ways. Even the vegetable that is a symbol of our national identity, the potato, arrived in Ireland from South America via Spanish explorers in the 1650s. The potato suited our soil and climate – plant a potato outside your door and in 13 to 20 weeks you'll have dinner – and quickly became our staple crop for generations. Potatoes were nutritious, providing potassium, vitamin C and D, and combined with buttermilk or milk in a pot and cooked over a fire with a little meat, they were the backbone of a good diet.

Fast forward to the 1970s, when the first signs of inward immigration were seen in the south of the country as a number of people, mainly German, Dutch and English, began to buy smallholdings, particularly around West Cork and Kerry. Many of these farmhouses had been abandoned during the Famine or the years following it. These are the people who looked at our produce with fresh eyes and fell in love with it. They began making cheeses and curing meats and can be credited with beginning the thriving farmhouse cheese culture we have today.

Cooking techniques haven't changed much over the years, but time started to become a major factor in how we cooked and ate. Pressure cookers became popular in the 1970s in an effort to reduce cooking times and to make mealtimes faster. By the 1980s a multitude of fast new cooking inventions were introduced, the microwave being the most significant, as cooking food quickly and conveniently started to become prioritised. Convenience food itself also started to appear in supermarkets, with quicker cooking times being the main selling point.

Let's jump again, this time to the 1990s, when our economy boomed. You could say that the launch of Ryanair played a huge role in changing our eating and cooking habits. The arrival of this low-cost airline meant that Irish people could now travel around Europe for as little as €10 and we went in droves, tasting our way around different cities and countries and bringing home an appetite to have these foods here too.

In 1994 we had full employment in Ireland for the first time in our history, and as a result we had inward immigration on a scale never seen before. In the past 30 years our population has changed monumentally, including a growing diversity in our food culture and a large increase in the number of cuisines available here. Most recently, West African, Filipino and Ukrainian food businesses have been springing up around the country.

These influences are reflected in the Irish kitchen and in the food that's put on the table. In 2020, Bord Bia (the Irish Food Board) published the findings of a major survey called 'What We Ate Last Night' in which they detailed the attitudes to cooking in Ireland and how things have changed. Factors such as responsible living, busier lives, technology devices, convenience food, home deliveries and mealtimes were all listed as influencing what is cooked for evening meals or how they are cooked. Interestingly, when it came to the type of food eaten, the majority of adults still claimed that the classic 'meat and two veg' is their favourite meal, while the most popular meal among Irish children was spaghetti Bolognese.

The changing diversity of the Irish population and our appetite for eating food we experience abroad on holidays mean that the food enjoyed at home in Ireland has changed too. Spag Bol isn't the only Italian dish to have been appropriated and welcomed at the Irish dinner table – lasagne is one of the most common Irish dinners too, so much so that Graham has included it as a classic Irish dish in this book on page 174. A plate of lasagne, coleslaw and chips does not exist outside of Ireland, yet when we discuss Irish food culture, this uniquely Irish combination can often be overlooked. The same can be said for the spice bag (page 180), taco fries, chicken fillet rolls (page 68) and chilli con carne. Although the latter was definitely not an Irish invention, we have adapted it to our tables and palates.

This book is the epitome of modern Irish food culture, showcasing classic dishes updated with modern twists, our traditional Irish mealtimes and the importance of family, heritage, ingredients and flavour. We are fortunate to be invited to dine at Graham's table through these recipes.

# Cooking

**A pinch, knob, glug, dash, sprinkle & handful**

- A **pinch** of something (usually referring to a spice or dried herbs) is approximately ¼ teaspoon, while a **good pinch** is ½ teaspoon.
- A **knob** usually refers to butter or solid fat and is about 25g.
- A **glug**, referring to oils, is about 1 tablespoon, whereas a **good glug** would be 2–3 tablespoons.
- A **dash** normally refers to a liquid like vinegar or alcohol that is added at the end of the cooking time or across the top of a finished dish.
- A **sprinkle** would usually be a good pinch (½ teaspoon) scattered across the top of a finished dish.
- A **handful** normally refers to fresh herbs. A **small handful** is usually a quarter of a standard pack of fresh herbs, a **handful** is half a pack and a **large handful** is most of the bag.

**Béchamel sauce** In my opinion, béchamel (white sauce) is the most versatile sauce. Using a classic béchamel as a base, you can make everything from a parsley sauce for bacon and cabbage to a velouté for something like the fish lasagne on page 178.

50g butter
50g plain flour
500ml milk
salt and freshly ground black pepper

Melt the butter in a heavy-based saucepan over a medium heat. When the butter is starting to foam, add the flour and cook for 1 minute. Whisk in one-quarter of the milk and cook, still whisking, for 2 minutes. Whisk in the rest of the milk and simmer for 5–8 minutes, whisking occasionally, until nicely thickened. Stir in any additional flavours (see below), then remove the pan from the heat and use as required.

**Cheese sauce:** Stir in 100g of grated cheese and 1 teaspoon of mustard for the last 2 minutes of the cooking time. This is perfect for the cauliflower cheese on page 136.

**Mushroom sauce:** Cook 100g of sliced mushrooms in butter over a high heat until they have wilted and taken on a little colour, then stir them into the sauce just before serving. This is a great sauce with a pork chop.

**Mustard sauce:** Stir in 1–2 tablespoons of a mustard of your choice just before serving. Great as an alternative sauce for bacon.

**Parsley sauce:** Stir in a small handful of finely chopped curly parsley for the last 3 minutes of the cooking time.

**Soubise sauce:** Slowly cook two thinly sliced onions in butter over a low heat for 30–40 minutes, stirring occasionally, until they are caramelised – yes, properly caramelised onions really do take that long. Stir the onions and all their butter into the sauce just before serving. The sauce can be blended with a hand blender or left chunky. This works well with the cabbage and bacon on page 86.

**Velouté:** Replace the milk with 500ml stock. Velouté is a great base for things like the filo pie on page 132 and the fish lasagne on page 178.

~~~~~~~~~~~~~~~~~~~~~~~~~~~~~~

**Dish sizes** Several times throughout this book I call for dishes to be cooked in an ovenproof dish. I have tried to use the same size dish in all the recipes: either a 25cm x 25cm square dish or a 30cm x 22cm rectangular dish. However, these sizes are interchangeable, so if the recipe calls for a square dish but you only have a rectangular one (or vice versa), that's fine.

~~~~~~~~~~~~~~~~~~~~~~~~~~~~~~

**Eggs** All eggs used in this book are medium and free range. Make sure your eggs are at room temperature before cooking.

**Boiled egg:** Bring a small pot of water to a boil, then slowly lower your eggs into the water using a large spoon. Cook as follows:
- 4–5 minutes for a runny yolk
- 6–7 minutes for a gooey egg yolk – this is how I like them for salads and sandwiches
- 7–8 minutes for hardboiled

**Fried egg:** Crack your egg onto a saucer. Heat 1 tablespoon of butter or oil in a frying pan over a medium-low heat. Gently slide the egg into the pan, reduce the heat to low, season with salt and pepper and cover the pan with a lid, then cook for 3 minutes. Make sure the white is set before serving – if not, just cook it a little longer. For sunny-side-up eggs, don't cover the pan with a lid. Allow the egg white to completely cook and the yolk to stay runny. It will probably get a little crisp around the edges, but that just adds to the flavour.

**Poached egg:** First make sure your eggs are as fresh as possible – this makes a huge difference when poaching eggs. Crack your egg into a small bowl, as this makes it much easier to add it to the water. Bring a saucepan of water to a gentle simmer and add a dash of white wine vinegar. Don't add any salt to the water, as it causes the egg white to break up. Stir the water to create a whirlpool, then gently pour in your egg. Simmer for 2 minutes, then turn off the heat and let the egg sit for a further 8–10 minutes to finish cooking. Remove with a slotted spoon and put on kitchen paper to remove any excess water, then season to taste.

**Scrambled egg:** See page 26.

~~~~~~~~~~~~~~~~~~~~~~~~~~~~~~

**Flatbreads** This quick flatbread is the perfect accompaniment for a lot of dishes in this book. Who doesn't like some fresh warm bread to scoop up their food or to mop up the last little bits on the plate? Think outside the box in terms of flavours and what you can use the flatbreads for. I've even made sage and onion flatbreads to have with a roast chicken dinner – gorgeous!

> **350g self-raising flour, plus extra for dusting**
> **350g Greek yogurt**
> **seasoning of choice – chopped scallions, za'atar, dried fruit and flaked almonds, fresh coriander and garlic, any other fresh herbs**

Put the flour, yogurt and seasonings in a large bowl and mix together with a knife to form a dough, adding a drop of water if the dough is too stiff. Dust a clean work surface with a little flour, then tip the dough out onto the counter and knead for a minute or so to bring it all together. Put the dough in a flour-dusted bowl, cover with a clean tea towel and leave to rest for 30 minutes at room temperature. Divide the dough in half, then divide each half into four equal-sized pieces to make eight flatbreads. Use a rolling pin to roll each piece into a 12cm round, roughly 3mm thick. Put a frying pan over a high heat without any oil. Once it's hot, add as many rounds as will fit in your pan without overcrowding it. Cook for 1–2 minutes on each side in the dry frying pan, until puffed up and colouring nicely, turning with tongs. Wrap the flatbreads in a clean tea towel to keep warm until ready to serve.

**Family-style dining** The communal nature of sharing dishes family style makes it easier to strike up a conversation, brings people together and creates a space to unite people. Simply put all the dishes you are going to share in the centre of the table and let everyone help themselves, although I do like the idea of somebody being 'Mammy' when it comes to serving the main component of the meal.

**Garlic butter** I always have a block of garlic butter on the go in the fridge. It's great for adding a quick bit of flavour to most dishes, from a pat on top of roast and fried meats to melting over some simple boiled vegetables. If you can get your hands on wild garlic during its season from mid-February to April, it makes a fantastic garlic butter.

200g salted butter, very soft
2 garlic cloves, finely chopped
2 tbsp finely chopped fresh parsley
freshy ground black pepper

In a bowl, mix the butter, garlic and parsley together with a little black pepper. When well combined, scrape the butter out onto a square of baking paper or cling film. Shape the butter into a sausage by rolling it up and twisting the ends to seal like a Christmas cracker and compact the butter, Keep the butter refrigerated until required and use within one week. The garlic butter can also be frozen. Once chilled, cut it into slices and put them on a baking tray lined with non-stick baking paper, then put the tray in the freezer. Once the slices are frozen, transfer them to a ziplock bag or freezerproof container and take out as needed. Allow to defrost at room temperature for half an hour before using. The butter will keep in the freezer for up to three months.

**Ginger** The easiest way to peel ginger is to scrape the skin off with the side of a spoon.

**Herbs** I recommend that everyone grows three herbs at home: bay leaves, rosemary and thyme. These are all sturdy plants that are happy with Irish weather and grow well in pots. To make fresh herbs like coriander, mint and parsley last longer, simply take them out of the packets when you get home from the shops, roll them up in a dampened sheet of kitchen paper and put them in a ziplock bag before refrigerating.

**The holy trinity** Lasagne, coleslaw and chips isn't the only holy trinity in cooking! You have probably chopped carrots, celery and onion countless times as a base for your cooking, but did you know that they are considered to be the foundation of flavour? I've used the combination lots of times throughout this book, along with garlic, as a base to build a dish on. It's such a classic that in some countries it's known by one word – in France it's a mirepoix, in Italy it's soffritto and in Germany it's Suppengrün.

The Germans use leek and celeriac instead of onions and celery, but the flavour profile is still the same.

~~~~~~~~~~~~~~~~~~~~~~~~~~~~

**Labneh** Labneh is basically a strained yogurt. Like most ingredients, use the best you can afford – the better the yogurt, the better and richer your labneh will be. Starting with 1kg of natural yogurt will yield roughly 500g of labneh.

> **1kg natural yogurt**
> **flavourings of choice**

Line a sieve with a double layer of muslin or cheesecloth and pour the yogurt into the centre. Gather the corners of the cloth together and tie with some kitchen string. The best way to drain the yogurt is to suspend it above a bowl in your fridge. If it's not possible to suspend it, simply leave it in the fridge sitting in the sieve above a bowl to drain. After 24 hours, remove the labneh from the cloth and flavour or use as required. The water that has drained off (the whey) can be used in the same way as buttermilk. I have a couple of ways I like to flavour labneh: garlic and chive, dill and black pepper, or the roast beetroot version on page 163.

~~~~~~~~~~~~~~~~~~~~~~~~~~~~

**Mash with butter ... or butter with mash**
Sometimes you need to have your mash with a little (or a lot!) more luxury, so here's a guide to how much butter and other liquids to add to your mashed potatoes based on using 1kg of potatoes to start with.

| Mash occasion | Liquid | Butter |
| --- | --- | --- |
| Monday–Thursday | 50ml milk | 25g butter |
| Friday & Saturday | 50ml milk | 75g butter |
| Sunday roast | 50ml cream | 25g butter and some juices from the roasting pan |

| Mash occasion | Liquid | Butter |
| --- | --- | --- |
| Special treat | 50ml cream | 100g butter |
| Extra-special | 100ml double cream | As much butter as you dare, up to 250g |

~~~~~~~~~~~~~~~~~~~~~~~~~~~~

**Mushrooms** Never wash mushrooms, as they will absorb too much water and will turn soggy, which makes them almost impossible to fry. Use a pastry brush to brush off any soil or debris.

~~~~~~~~~~~~~~~~~~~~~~~~~~~~

**Oil** I use vegetable oil in many recipes throughout this book, but feel free to use whichever type of oil you prefer, whether that's sunflower, rapeseed or olive oil. When it comes to drizzling oil over finished dishes, use the best extra-virgin olive oil you can – it really makes a difference.

~~~~~~~~~~~~~~~~~~~~~~~~~~~~

**Old Bay seasoning** Originating in Baltimore, Maryland, this spice blend that's heavy on the celery salt and paprika is traditionally used to flavour crab, prawns and other seafood. I use it on chips, corn on the cob and eggs. If you can't find it in the shops, here's my version.

> **1 tbsp celery salt**
> **1 tbsp sweet paprika**
> **1 tbsp smoked paprika**
> **1 tsp mustard powder**
> **1 tsp ground black pepper**
> **1 tsp ground white pepper**
> **½ tsp ground nutmeg**
> **½ tsp ground cinnamon**
> **4 whole cloves**
> **3 dried bay leaves**

Put everything in a spice mill and grind together. Transfer to a sealed glass jar and store in a cool, dark place for up to six months.

~~~~~~~~~~~~~~~~~~~~~~~~~~~~

**Oven temperatures** Always preheat your oven. All the temperatures in the recipes in this book are based on a fan-assisted Celsius oven, but it may help to have these conversions.

| Celsius (fan assisted) | Celsius | Fahrenheit | Gas mark |
|---|---|---|---|
| 100°C | 110°C | 225°F | ¼ |
| 120°C | 130°C | 250°F | ½ |
| 130°C | 140°C | 275°F | 1 |
| 140°C | 150°C | 300°F | 2 |
| 155°C | 170°C | 325°F | 3 |
| 165°C | 180°C | 350°F | 4 |
| 180°C | 190°C | 375°F | 5 |
| 190°C | 200°C | 400°F | 6 |
| 200°C | 220°C | 425°F | 7 |
| 210°C | 230°C | 450°F | 8 |
| 220°C | 240°C | 475°F | 9 |

〜〜〜〜〜〜〜〜〜〜〜〜〜〜〜〜

**Potatoes: Floury, waxy & all-rounders** It can be a bit of a minefield knowing which potato is best for which dish, but please do try to seek out some of the more unusual varieties. If all else fails, just grab a bag of Ireland's most popular potato, the Rooster.

| Type | Name | Boil | Mash | Roast | Chip | Bake | Salad |
|---|---|---|---|---|---|---|---|
| Floury | Maris Piper, King Edward, Golden Wonder | | ✳ | ✳ | ✳ | ✳ | |
| Waxy | Pink Fir Apple, Charlotte | | | ✳ | | | ✳ |
| All-rounder | Rooster, Yukon Gold | ✳ | ✳ | ✳ | ✳ | ✳ | ✳ |

〜〜〜〜〜〜〜〜〜〜〜〜〜〜〜〜

**Ras el hanout** I visited Morocco again while I was writing this book. I stayed in a riad in Essaouira and spent the days wandering the narrow streets of the citadel. The streets were packed with shops selling everything from carpets to pottery, not to mention the countless food stands, from producers making homemade amlou (an almond butter with argan oil and honey) and carts filled with prickly pears to stands with the most beautiful fresh herbs and vegetables, stalls with terracotta urns filled with olives and preserved lemons and last but not least, my favourite: the spice sellers. I discovered a spice seller in the fish market called Chez Makki and saw that he was grinding the spices to order. I asked for some ras el hanout, and in the blink of an eye he was darting around the shop gathering whole spices out of jars. I was no longer the kid in Keane's sweet shop ordering a quarter – I was an adult in a spice shop ordering my own spice blend, but the feeling was the same: one of wonder, excitement and anticipation. Before I knew it, he had handed me my bag of freshly ground spices. The whole process happened so fast that I was completely overwhelmed, so I went back the following day to order some more, but this time I brought a pen and paper. I was a man on a mission to learn from a master. I think he got a kick out of this overly excited man wanting to know so much about his spices. And what I learned that day blew my mind. His ras el hanout contains a mix of 13 spices: cinnamon, star anise, nutmeg, mace, green cardamon, dried ginger, juniper berries, galangal, bay leaves, turmeric and three different types of pepper (black, green and long pepper). I don't expect you to go out and get 13 different spices to make that same blend, so if you can't get it ready made, here's a simpler recipe.

> 2 tbsp cumin seeds
> 2 tbsp coriander seeds
> 2 tbsp coriander seeds
> 2 tbsp cumin seeds
> 2 tsp ground ginger
> 2 tsp black peppercorns
> 1 tsp ground turmeric
> 1 cinnamon stick
> seeds from 12 green cardamon pods

Put everything in a spice mill and grind it all together. Transfer to a sealed glass jar and store in a cool, dark place for up to six months.

〜〜〜〜〜〜〜〜〜〜〜〜〜〜〜〜

**Relax & rest** Not only is this good advice for us because daily life can be full of challenges, demands and deadlines, but it's even better advice for your meat. Any meat that has been fried or roasted will benefit from a rest because it gives the muscle fibres a chance to relax and the juices a chance to redistribute. Simply cover the meat lightly with a sheet of foil and put a clean tea towel on top. It will sit comfortably like this for 10–20 minutes depending on the size of the piece of meat.

**Salt & freshly ground black pepper** Food needs salt. I've spent most of my working life in the sweeter side of catering, where, yes, salt is used and even pepper occasionally. Over time I had forgotten the joy of good seasoning, particularly the joy of pepper. My seasoning tray has grown and now consists of the following:

**Fine/table salt:** Use when seasoning water that is going to have something like veg or pasta cooked in it.

**A salt mill filled with coarse sea salt:** This is my main go-to salt seasoning, used for everything from seasoning eggs to stews.

**Flaky sea salt:** Great for finishing dishes and sprinkled on food at the last moment, like steak. My personal favourites are Achill Sea Salt and West of Dingle Sea Salt.

**Onion salt:** A recent discovery and a revelation.

**Black pepper mill:** You can't beat freshly ground black pepper.

**White pepper mill:** For years I only ever had Saxa ground white pepper but grinding your own will blow your mind! The flavour and freshness are addictive.

**Saxa black and white pepper:** Sometimes only the original will do.

**Mixed peppercorns:** I like to crush these in a pestle and mortar to season things like steaks and roast meats.

**Salt & vinegar seasoning** I always have a little jar of this on the go. Great for sprinkling on chips, crisps and fried fish.

> 5 tbsp fine salt
> 3 tbsp malt vinegar
> 2 tbsp cornflour

Make a paste out of all the ingredients and spread it out on a baking sheet lined with baking parchment. Leave at room temperature, uncovered, for three to five days to completely dry out, then break up the salt and crush it with the back of a spoon. Store in an airtight container and use as required.

**Scallions, green onions & spring onions** Did you know there is a difference between scallions, green onions and spring onions? What we get most commonly in shops in Ireland are scallions. If the scallion is allowed to form a bulb at its base, it's technically a green onion. Both the green and white parts of a scallion and green onion are edible. Spring onions are completely different – they are basically very young regular onions and most of the green parts are inedible.

**Shallow-frying** Quite a few recipes in this book call for shallow frying, so here are a few tips:

- Heat the oil in a deep frying pan. DO NOT heat the pan and then add the oil when shallow-frying, as the oil heats more evenly when heated in a cold pan.
- Be very careful when placing food into the pan – lay it down away from you to avoid splashes.
- Don't overcrowd the pan when cooking.
- Use tongs to turn food – they will give you more control than a spoon or spatula.
- Listen to the food: the sound of the food frying will get quieter as it reaches the point of being cooked.
- Look at the food: the bubbles around the food will lessen as it reaches the point of being done.
- Be very careful when removing food from the pan and put it on kitchen paper to absorb excess oil.
- Keep fried food warm while cooking any remaining items.
- Never leave a frying pan with oil unattended on the hob.

**Sterilising glass jars** Sterilising glass jars helps to extend the life of whatever food you're putting in the jars by killing any potential bacteria.

- Preheat the oven to 120°C fan.
- Wash your glass jars and metal lids thoroughly in warm soapy water and rinse completely.
- Put the clean glass jars on a baking tray and put them in the oven for 10 minutes.
- Put the lids in a saucepan of boiling water for 3 minutes.

**Stock** Yes, homemade stock is best, but let's be realistic – most people are not going to make stock at home. As with all food, buy the best you can afford. Pouches of fresh stock are now available in most supermarkets as well as stock jellies, bouillons and of course good old stock cubes. Having said that, though, both chicken and vegetable stock are really easy to make. I keep a large ziplock bag in my freezer and whenever I have vegetable trimmings or peelings, I add them to the bag. When the bag is full, I make a vegetable stock by frying all the vegetable bits in a little vegetable oil in a large saucepan for a few minutes, then adding enough cold water to cover and a bay leaf. Bring to a boil, then reduce the heat and simmer for 1½ hours. Pass through a sieve and use as required. If I have the carcass of a roast chicken, I will make a chicken stock in a similar way. Also, when you're on a foreign holiday, check out the stock cubes in supermarkets – I've brought home red wine stock cubes from France and tom yum ones from Thailand!

# Break

# fast

# Porridge

Porridge. The word alone has such negative connotations: a bowl of grey, gloopy slop associated with poverty, hunger, suffering and even prison. Yet we must be able and allowed to acknowledge and embrace our food history in order to move forward with our food future. Porridge sustained many people during hard times and I believe it should be celebrated. So whether it's hot, cold, sweet or even savoury, let's welcome the humble oatmeal into our lives and honour it by making it delicious.

Call me Goldilocks, but I don't like my day-to-day porridge too hot or too cold, too sweet or too salty. I like it just right, and with a little practice, you will get your porridge just right too. It's a different story at the weekends or a day off, when you can take it to the next level – see the variations on pages 22–23.

Serves 2

80g porridge oats/ oatmeal (see the note)

550ml liquid (water, milk or half water, half milk – see the note)

a pinch of salt

The night before, put the oats and half of the liquid in a saucepan, cover and allow to soak. If you're using all milk, put the saucepan in the fridge. If you're using water, it's okay to leave it out.

In the morning, add the remaining liquid and a pinch of salt.

Slowly bring to a boil on a medium heat, then allow to simmer gently for 6–8 minutes, stirring occasionally so that it doesn't stick to the bottom of the pan.

To serve, divide between two warm bowls and top as desired. Here are some suggestions:

- Honey and cinnamon – my go-to daily topping

- Whipped cream, a dash of Irish cream liqueur and milk chocolate chips

- A teaspoon of rosewater, fresh figs and chopped pistachios

- Banana, maple syrup and roast pecans

- Raspberries and white chocolate chips

## Note

Use jumbo oats or rolled oats if you prefer a chunkier texture or porridge oats for a finer, smoother texture. You can use water, milk or half water, half milk. My preferred method is to soak the oats in water and then finish cooking them in milk.

# Variations

## OATRAGEOUS!

**CARROT CAKE PORRIDGE WITH ORANGE CREAM CHEESE**
Add two grated carrots, 1 tablespoon maple syrup,
1 teaspoon ground cinnamon, 1 teaspoon vanilla bean
paste and 20g sultanas (optional) at the cooking stage.
When serving, spoon on some crème fraîche that has had
some orange zest and vanilla bean paste mixed through.
Finally, top with chopped roasted pecans.

## SAVOURY MUSHROOM & EGG PORRIDGE

Replace the soaking water and the milk in the cooking with chicken or vegetable stock. When cooked, top with sautéed mushrooms which have had some miso paste added for extra umami flavour, a warm soft-boiled egg (see page 11) and slivers of spring onion. A little hot sauce would also be a good accompaniment if you want to spice things up a little.

## OVERNIGHT OATS

Start the night before, as they are overnight oats! In a suitable storage container (my preferred choice is a Kilner jar), stir 50g of porridge oats into 100ml of water or milk (or 50ml of each) along with ¼ teaspoon ground cinnamon and store in the fridge overnight. The following morning, loosen the oats with a little more liquid if required before topping with natural yogurt, a drizzle of honey and fresh berries.

# Homemade granola

Granola is one of those great recipes that allows you to make it personal. This is my version and is filled with all the things I love in a breakfast cereal, leaving out all the nasties. Don't get me wrong, I love sultanas, walnuts and desiccated coconut – just not in my granola. But if you want them, add them! If you want to make this vegan, just replace the honey with something like agave syrup and the dried figs with other dried fruits. I like to eat granola with Greek yogurt and fresh blueberries, but again, make it personal with plant-based milks, other yogurt and different fresh fruit. Try sprinkling a little granola on top of a warm bowl of porridge to add a little crunch.

Makes 750g

120ml honey

40g coconut oil

½ tsp salt

340g jumbo oats

150g nuts (I like pistachios, pecans and almonds)

100g mixed seeds (pumpkin and sunflower)

50g coconut flakes

100g finely chopped dried fruit (apricots, figs and cranberries)

Preheat the oven to 150°C fan. Line a baking tray with non-stick baking paper.

Gently heat the honey, oil and salt together in a small pan over a low heat until the oil has melted. Allow to cool slightly.

Mix the oats, nuts, seeds and coconut flakes in a large bowl. Stir the honey and oil into the dry mix and combine well. I like to use my hands at this stage as that way I can make sure everything is really well coated with the oil and honey.

Spread out on the baking tray and bake in the preheated oven for 30–35 minutes, until golden, stirring every 10 minutes to make sure it toasts and colours evenly.

Remove from the oven and let the granola cool and crisp up on the tray, then stir in the dried fruit. Store in an airtight container for up to six weeks.

# Smoked salmon & scrambled eggs

The warm creaminess of freshly scrambled eggs against the cold, silky smoked salmon is an amazing combination, but we can take it one step further. I love it served on a slice of toasted brown soda bread with a scattering of chives, a wedge of lemon and lots of freshly ground black pepper across the top. The sweetness of the bread, that mild allium flavour of the chives, the sharpness of the lemon and the earthy, hot hit of black pepper take this dish from amazing to phenomenal.

Serves 2

6 medium free-range eggs

1 tbsp crème fraîche

salt and freshy ground black pepper

2 slices of brown soda bread

30g butter, plus extra for the toast

4 slices of smoked salmon

finely chopped fresh chives

1 lemon, cut into wedges

Crack the eggs into a bowl. Add the crème fraîche, season with salt and a little black pepper and gently whisk together.

Put your bread on to toast.

Melt the butter in a non-stick frying pan over a medium heat until it starts to foam. Add the eggs and let the mixture sit for about 15 seconds, then using a spatula, gently move the eggs around the pan. Let the mixture sit again for about 15 seconds, then stir. Repeat until the eggs are softly set and still a little wet, as the eggs will continue to cook for another minute or so off the heat.

To serve, butter your toasted bread, give the eggs one final stir and spoon them over the toast. Drape the salmon over the eggs and finish with a scattering of finely chopped fresh chives, an extra grind of black pepper and a wedge of lemon to squeeze over.

# Hot smoked salmon & baked eggs

There are food pairings that we all know and love: strawberries and cream, peanut butter and jam, rhubarb and custard, fish and chips. And then there are food pairings that are a bit more out there, that shouldn't make sense but do, like buttermilk and potatoes (page 140), beans and coffee (page 164) and in this recipe, horseradish (which is usually served with beef) and smoked fish. What makes food pairings work is their contrasts: sweet and salty, hot and cold, sour and creamy – or in this case, the spiciness of the horseradish and the smooth creaminess of the baked smoked salmon and crème fraîche.

Serves 2

butter, for greasing

80g smoked salmon

80g crème fraîche

1–2 tsp horseradish sauce, depending on how much of a kick you would like

1 sprig of fresh parsley, finely chopped

salt and freshly ground black pepper

2 eggs

1 tbsp finely grated Parmesan cheese (which is usually reserved for beef)

**To garnish:**

finely chopped fresh parsley

**To serve:**

buttered Guinness brown bread

Preheat the oven to 180°C fan. Grease two ovenproof ramekins and bring a full kettle to a boil.

Divide the smoked salmon between the two greased ramekins.

In a separate bowl, combine the crème fraiche, horseradish and most of the parsley and season with a little salt and ground black pepper. Divide between the two ramekins.

Crack an egg into each ramekin and top with a little more parsley and the Parmesan. Put the ramekins in an ovenproof baking dish. Pour the just-boiled water from the kettle into the dish until it comes halfway up the sides of the ramekins. Bake in the preheated oven for 15–18 minutes, until the egg whites are set and the yolks are still soft.

Scatter over a pinch of finely chopped fresh parsley and serve with the buttered Guinness brown bread from my first book, *Bake*, cut into fingers if you like for dipping into the warm egg and the crème fraiche.

# Prunes & yogurt

You're getting a two-for-one here, as these Earl Grey-soaked prunes are a fantastic breakfast but they also work well as a simple dessert. When I was growing up these would have regularly been on the table at home and in my Granny Daisy's but served with custard. I like to serve them for breakfast at room temperature with thick, cold Greek yogurt, a little honey and toasted almonds.

Makes 2 jars

200g dried prunes

2 strips of orange rind

1 vanilla pod, cut in half lengthways

1 cinnamon stick, broken in half

2 Earl Grey tea bags

50g caster sugar

250ml water

**To serve:**

Greek yogurt (or warm custard if you fancy them for dessert)

toasted flaked almonds

honey

Divide the prunes between two sterile jars (see page 17). Add one strip of orange rind, half the vanilla pod and one piece of cinnamon to each jar.

Put the tea bags, sugar and water in a saucepan and bring to a boil, then reduce the heat and simmer for 5 minutes. Discard the tea bags before dividing the liquid between the two jars.

Allow to infuse and soak for three days before eating. Serve in a bowl with some yogurt, toasted flaked almonds and honey. Alternatively, serve the prunes ice cold in a warm bowl of custard – a childhood favourite of mine.

# Melon, avocado, crème fraîche & pine nuts

I have Mrs Mary Bowe of Marlfield House to thank for introducing me to this combination. It was on the breakfast menu when I was working there back in the late 1990s and it's still one of my favourites. Marlfield House was an amazing place to work where the attention to detail was second to none. The house had a stunning state room, their own vegetable and herb garden, a peacock roaming the grounds and two house dogs, Elizabeth and Buttons, wandering about. It was, and still is, a magical place.

Do try to plan this one in advance to give your melon and avocados time to come to ripe perfection. My personal choice of melon for this dish is cantaloupe but honeydew, Galia or canary also work well. And while I sing the praises of Irish dairy from the rooftops and use it wherever I can, on this occasion, if you can source French crème fraîche, in particular Isigny Sainte-Mère AOP, go for it – you won't regret it.

Serves 2

50g pine nuts

½ ripe melon (see the intro), peeled, deseeded and sliced

1 ripe avocado, halved, stoned and sliced

2 generous tbsp crème fraîche

a drizzle of extra-virgin olive oil (optional)

Toast the pine nuts in a dry frying pan over a medium heat, stirring or shaking the pan until they are golden brown. Allow to cool before using.

Simply divide the melon and avocado between two serving plates and top each one with a generous tablespoon of crème fraîche, a scattering of toasted pine nuts and a drizzle of extra-virgin olive oil (if using).

# Full Irish

I recently asked 'What should be in a traditional Irish fry?' on social media. Of course, there are the givens: sausage,* bacon, pudding** and egg. Also, it goes without saying that a full Irish should be served with copious amounts of tea,*** hot toast and real butter.

What I wasn't expecting from the replies to my question was the outrage and disdain that some people have for the trimmings. I never knew that tomatoes, beans, hash browns and mushrooms could cause so much consternation, but at the end of the day (or should I say at the beginning of the day?), it's your breakfast – have what you like!

Serves 4

## The rules

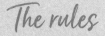

\* **Pork sausages - never, EVER anything else**

\*\* **Black and/or white, but a traditional Irish fry must have pudding**

\*\*\* **Must be Barry's or Lyons!**

**The essentials:**

vegetable oil

8 pork sausages

8 slices of black and/
or white pudding

8 rashers (I love both
plain back rashers
and smoked streaky
rashers)

eggs, cooked to your
liking (see page 11)

**The add-ons:**

2 tomatoes

1 x 415g tin of baked
beans

hash browns, fresh
(page 38) or frozen

mushrooms

cooked and cooled
potatoes, roughly
chopped

vegetable oil

butter

salt and freshly
ground black pepper

dried thyme

**To serve:**

lots of tea

toast or brown bread

butter

The best tip I can give you for cooking a full Irish is to preheat the oven to a low setting, about 100°C fan. This will act as a hot-hold where you can put each of the different bits as you cook them, enabling you to serve everything warm at the end. If you're cooking the tomatoes or the hash browns, simply cook these at the temperature stated and then turn off the oven, as the residual heat will be more than enough to keep everything warm. And don't forget to warm your plates in the oven to help keep your breakfast warm.

**Sausages:** Heat a little vegetable oil in a large frying pan over a medium heat. Add the sausages and cook for about 10 minutes, turning occasionally, until brown all over and completely cooked through. Keep warm in the oven.

**Pudding:** Slice the pudding and cook in the frying pan for a few minutes on each side until crisp and heated all the way through. Keep warm in the oven.

**Bacon:** Fry or grill the rashers to your liking. I like mine a little crispy. Keep warm in the oven.

**Tomatoes:** Preheat the oven to 180°C fan. Cut each tomato in half and put in a baking dish, cut side up. Put a little knob of butter on top of each half, season with salt and pepper and a small pinch of dried thyme. Bake in the preheated oven for 15–20 minutes.

**Beans:** Open a tin of beans, tip them into a saucepan and heat – or see pages 166–167 to bring your beans to the next level.

**Hash browns:** Cook as per the packet instructions if using frozen ones or as per the recipe on page 38 if making homemade hash browns.

**Mushrooms:** Clean your mushrooms by using a pastry brush to brush off any soil that may still be attached. Depending on the size of your mushrooms, cut each one in half or quarters. Heat 1 tablespoon of vegetable oil and a knob of butter in a saucepan over a medium heat. Once the butter is foaming, add the mushrooms but resist the urge to stir them. Allow them to fry a little before shaking the pan and again allowing the mushrooms to fry undisturbed. Continue doing this for about 10 minutes. If the mushrooms release a lot of moisture, simply turn up the heat and allow the moisture to evaporate, then turn down the heat and fry a little. Season with salt and black pepper.

**Fried potatoes:** I like to add a little butter to either the sausage or bacon frying pan to fry my potatoes. All the little bits on the bottom of the pan as well as the juices from frying are full of flavour that deserve to be used. Add the potatoes and fry over a medium heat until golden all over. Season with salt and pepper. Keep warm in the oven.

Serve everything with eggs of your choice, tea and toast.

# Hash browns, coffee bacon & brown butter eggs

I don't think it's blood that runs through my veins, it's bacon! In the same way a lot of people think that a cup of tea can solve the world's problems, I think a slice of bacon can do the same thing. I'm not sure if it's my German ancestry, if it's because my father, my grandfather and even my great-grandfather were all pork butchers or if it's simply the fact that a warm slice of streaky bacon, with its crispy, salty, juicy and fatty texture, can give you the best mouthfeel ever. Mouthfeel is a word I'm not overly fond of but I have yet to find a word that better explains the taste, texture, chemical reaction and transformation that goes on in your mouth when you eat something you love.

Serves 4

**For the coffee bacon:**

12 slices of thick streaky bacon, smoked or unsmoked

4 tbsp espresso or strong coffee, cooled

2 tbsp maple syrup

a pinch of smoked paprika

**To garnish:**

finely chopped fresh chives

The day before you want to serve this, lay the bacon on a baking tray lined with non-stick baking paper. Mix the coffee, maple syrup and smoked paprika together and brush it over the bacon, making sure each piece is covered. Cover with cling film and put in the fridge overnight.

The next day, preheat the oven to 180°C fan.

To make the hash browns, coarsely grate the potatoes and the onion into the middle of a clean tea towel, gather the corners of the towel together and squeeze out all the excess water. Tip the dried mixture out into a large bowl, crack in the egg and season generously with salt and pepper. Using your hands, mix well before shaping into four round patties about 2cm thick.

Before cooking the hash browns, remove the bacon from its coffee marinade (keep the marinade!), put the bacon on a new baking tray lined with a fresh sheet of non-stick baking paper and cook in the preheated oven for 8 minutes. Turn the bacon over and brush with the reserved marinade, then cook for a further 8 minutes. ➔

**For the hash browns:**

4 medium floury potatoes, such as Maris Pipers, unpeeled and scrubbed

1 medium onion

1 egg

salt and freshly ground black pepper

4 tbsp vegetable oil

**For the brown butter eggs:**

1 tbsp vegetable oil

50g butter

4 eggs

Meanwhile, heat the oil in a large non-stick frying pan over a medium-high heat. Carefully add the hash brown patties to the pan and fry for 3–4 minutes on each side, until crisp and browned all over. Keep warm while you cook the eggs.

To cook the brown butter eggs, heat the oil in a large frying pan over a high heat until it's very hot. Add the butter and turn the heat down to medium. The butter should be foaming and should turn brown but be careful not to let it burn. Gently crack each egg into the pan, season with salt and pepper, baste the top of each egg with some of the foaming butter and cover the pan with a lid for 3 minutes. Make sure the whites are set before serving – if they're not, give them a little more time.

To serve, put a hash brown on a warmed plate, top with a brown butter egg and sprinkle over finely chopped chives to garnish. Add coffee bacon on the side and enjoy, with a big mug of coffee.

# Soda farls

Warm, fluffy bread in less than 25 minutes – what could be better? Well, warm, fluffy bread with butter!

These simple breads make a great accompaniment to a full Irish (page 34) or you can fill them with bacon and tomato ketchup. They are also a great carrier of flavour – check out my modern version of this Irish classic on the next page to see how simple it is to add flavour to this bake.

Makes 4 farls

250g plain flour, plus extra for dusting

1 rounded tsp bread soda

1 tsp caster sugar

½ tsp salt

200ml buttermilk

25g butter, melted and cooled

Heat a large heavy-based frying pan over a medium-low heat.

Put the flour, bread soda, sugar and salt in a large bowl and mix together. Make a well in the centre of the flour, then quickly and gently add the buttermilk and melted butter. Mix together using a table knife to form a dough, then gently bring the dough together using your hands. Shape it into a 20cm round and use a sharp knife to cut the dough into quarters, or farls.

Add the farls to the hot, dry pan and cook on the medium-low heat for 10–12 minutes on each side, until golden brown on both sides and cooked through. Remove from the heat when cooked and allow to stand for 10 minutes.

Serve warm, cut in half and spread with lots of butter.

# Chicken & farls

This is my version of chicken and waffles, an American dish that has become a popular brunch option here in recent years. I first had it for breakfast many years ago, I think in 2002, when I went to New York with my sister, her husband and my niece Ellen. I absolutely loved the breakfast diner culture and the retro feel of some of the diners, but I especially loved all the lingo: hash, sunny-side-up, lox, high and dry, lumberjack, deluxe.

Serves 4

**For the spice blend:**

1 chicken stock cube, crumbled (Oxo works best)

2 tbsp paprika

2 tsp garlic granules

1 tsp onion salt

1 tsp dried oregano

1 tsp ground white pepper

½ tsp chilli powder

**For the chicken:**

250ml buttermilk

8 boneless, skinless chicken thighs

sunflower oil, for shallow-frying

125g plain flour

40g cornflour

Make the spice blend by mixing all the ingredients together in a small bowl.

In a bowl or baking dish, mix the buttermilk and 2 teaspoons of the spice blend together, then add the chicken, making sure it's all submerged in the buttermilk. Cover with cling film and marinate overnight in the fridge. Store the remaining spice mix in an airtight container.

The next day, make the hot honey butter by gently warming all the ingredients in a saucepan over a low heat with 1 teaspoon of the spice blend until the butter has melted and warmed slightly. Remove the pan from the heat and keep warm while you make the rest of the dish.

To make the farls, heat a large heavy-based frying pan over a medium-low heat.

Put the flour, bread soda, sugar and salt in a large bowl and whisk to combine, then stir in the spring onions, chilli and coriander. Make a well in the centre of the flour, then quickly add the buttermilk and olive oil. Mix together using a table knife to form a dough, then gently bring the dough together using your hands. Shape it into a 20cm round and use a sharp knife to cut the dough into quarters, or farls.

Add the farls to the hot, dry pan and cook on the medium-low heat for 10–12 minutes on each side, until golden brown on both sides and cooked through. Remove from the heat when cooked and set aside while you cook the chicken. ⊙

**For the hot honey butter:**

85g honey

60g butter

1 fresh red chilli, left whole and pierced with the tip of a sharp knife a few times

**For the farls:**

250g plain flour, plus extra for dusting

1 rounded tsp bread soda

1 tsp caster sugar

½ tsp salt

3 spring onions, finely chopped

1 small fresh red chilli, deseeded and finely chopped

1 small bunch of fresh coriander, finely chopped (reserve some for garnish)

200ml buttermilk

25ml olive oil

**To garnish:**

sliced fresh red chilli

flaky sea salt

Using a deep frying pan, add enough oil for shallow-frying (see page 17) and heat it over a medium-high heat.

To make the coating for the chicken, mix the flour and cornflour with 2 tablespoons of the spice blend in a wide, shallow bowl. Remove the chicken from the marinade but keep the marinade. Working with one chicken thigh at a time, coat the chicken by dipping it in the flour mixture. Use your fingers to make sure there is a nice thick layer of the coating on the chicken. Put each piece of chicken on a large board or plate while you prepare the rest.

Working with four pieces at a time, gently and carefully lower the chicken into the hot oil in the frying pan, making sure you lower it in away from you to avoid splashes. Cook for 4–5 minutes on each side, until completely cooked through. Keep the first batch of chicken warm while you cook the rest.

To serve, cut a farl in half and put the bottom on a serving plate. Top with two pieces of chicken, some slivers of fresh red chilli, chopped fresh coriander, a pinch of flaky salt and a drizzle of the hot honey butter. Add the top of the farl and serve with more of the hot honey butter.

# Lunch

# Ham & cheese toastie

Whether it's toasted sourdough with shredded ham hock and farmhouse cheese, a simple ham and cheese from your toasted sandwich maker at home or the classic toasted special from your local pub, we all love a toastie. Who remembers the good old days when your pub toastie would come in a special little plastic bag? My preference is for a pan-fried toastie with thick slices of ham, a little mustard, a few crispy onions and a mix of Cheddar and mozzarella, the latter adding that oozy, cheesy goodness. If you have any béchamel left over from any other recipe, it will bring this toastie to the next level.

Makes 1

2 slices of bread (my preference is fresh sourdough)

a smear of mustard

a couple of slices of cooked ham

a scattering of crispy onions

cheese of your choice (I like a mix of Cheddar and mozzarella), grated or thinly sliced

2 tbsp béchamel sauce (page 10; optional)

soft butter

Smear one slice of bread with a layer of mustard, then top with slices of ham and a few crispy onions. Put your cheese on top of the ham and onions. If using the béchamel, spread it on the second slice of bread and put this on top of the cheese, sauce facing the cheese.

Put your frying pan on a medium heat.

Spread the top of the sandwich with some soft butter and carefully place it in the frying pan, buttered side down. Gently cook for 5–6 minutes, turning the heat down if the bread is colouring too quickly.

Before flipping the toastie over, spread the top of the second side of the sandwich with more soft butter. Flip it over and cook for 5–6 minutes more. You want your sandwich to be golden brown and the cheese to be melted.

## Note

Try these delicious combinations:

- Smoked cheese and kimchi
- Emmental cheese, crispy bacon and a scattering of caraway seeds
- Mozzarella, tomato and pesto
- Brie and cranberry sauce

# White pudding toast

When I told my publisher about this recipe, she said, 'Only a butcher's son would think of this!' It's probably true. Not an hour goes by that I'm not thinking about food – and I'm not just thinking about what my next meal will be. I love thinking about the flavour, texture, smell and appearance of food. I'm aways wondering what other way I can use an ingredient or how can I change a dish to give it my twist. Yes, the butcher's son and the chef in me is always thinking of different ways to use ingredients, but it's the slightly more eccentric side of me that really likes to shake things up. In this case, I've taken one of my favourite Chinese takeaway dishes, prawn toast, and given it an Irish twist.

Makes 4

200g white pudding

1 egg

2 scallions, finely chopped, plus extra sliced scallions to garnish

4 slices of stale bread (I like to use sourdough)

2 tbsp tomato relish, plus extra to serve

100g sesame seeds

vegetable oil, for shallow-frying

Put the white pudding and egg in a food processor and pulse a few times to make a paste. Depending on the consistency of your pudding, you might be able to do this in a small bowl with a fork or you may need to add a few drops of water to the processor to help it blend into a paste. Transfer the paste to a bowl and stir in the chopped scallions.

Spread each slice of bread with a little tomato relish, then divide the pudding mixture among the four slices. Use a palette knife to spread out the pudding mixture evenly all the way to the edges of the bread.

Spread out the sesame seeds on a plate. Working with one piece of bread at a time, put the pudding side of each slice in the sesame seeds, gently pressing the back of the bread to make sure the sesame seeds stick to the pudding. Put the slice of bread on a clean board while you prepare the remaining slices.

Heat a frying pan over a medium-low heat and add enough oil to shallow-fry the bread (see page 17). Working in batches so that you don't overcrowd the pan and starting on the sesame side, add each slice to the hot pan and fry for 3–5 minutes on each side, until golden brown all over and the white pudding paste is cooked thorough. Put the cooked toast on a sheet of kitchen paper and keep warm while you cook the rest.

I like to serve these with a little extra tomato relish on the side and some sliced scallions scattered over.

# Vegetable soup & porridge bread

I have made this soup countless times throughout my career and often refer to it as hotel soup, as it always seems to be served in hotels for everything from weddings to funerals. It's probably one of the most versatile recipes in the book. It works just as well when using those odds and ends from the drawer of doom at the bottom of the fridge or if you are making a special soup for a family celebration or dinner party. See the next page for some unusual combinations and serving suggestions. I'm serving the soup with one of my favourite (and easiest) bread recipes.

Serves 2

40g butter or 2 tbsp vegetable oil

2 medium onions, diced

3 garlic cloves, finely chopped

350g mixed vegetables, peeled and diced (I've used carrots and celery in this version)

350g potatoes, peeled and diced

800ml chicken or vegetable stock

4 tbsp cream, plus extra to serve (optional)

salt and freshly ground black pepper

**To garnish:**

chopped fresh parsley

a pinch of paprika

To make the porridge bread, preheat the oven to 175°C fan. Grease a 2lb loaf tin and line with non-stick baking paper.

Combine the yogurt, egg and milk in a large bowl. Stir in the oats, bread soda, salt and three-quarters of the pumpkin seeds, mix well and transfer to the prepared loaf tin. Sprinkle the remaining pumpkin seeds on top.

Bake in the preheated oven for 45–55 minutes, until a skewer inserted into the centre of the bread comes out clean. Remove the loaf from the tin and leave to cool on a wire rack.

While the bread is baking, make the soup. Melt the butter or heat the oil in a large saucepan over a medium heat. Add the onions and cook for 5 minutes, stirring occasionally, before adding the garlic and cooking for a further 3 minutes. Add the mixed vegetables and cook for 5 minutes.

Add the potatoes and stock and bring to a simmer. Continue to simmer for 15–20 minutes, until the vegetables and potatoes are tender.

Using a hand blender, blend the soup till smooth. Add the cream (if using) and heat gently. Season with salt and pepper.

Serve in warm bowls with an extra drizzle of cream (if using) and a pinch of chopped fresh parsley and paprika, with slices of the porridge bread on the side.

For the porridge bread
(makes 1 loaf):

butter, for greasing

1 x 500g tub of full- or
low-fat natural yogurt

1 egg, beaten

3 tbsp milk

350g porridge oats

2 tsp bread soda

½ tsp salt

50g pumpkin seeds

# Variations

## I'M A SOUPERFAN!

### CURRIED PARSNIP & APPLE
Add 1 heaped tablespoon of curry powder to the vegetable soup on page 54 when cooking the onions. Use only diced parsnip and some celery when making up the 350g of vegetables. When reheating the soup after blending it, add two peeled and finely diced apples.

### BROCCOLI, BLUE CHEESE & ALMOND
Use both the florets and stalks of your broccoli to make up the 350g of vegetables. Garnish with crumbled blue cheese and toasted flaked almonds.

### CELERIAC & HAZELNUT
Use peeled, diced celeriac to make up the 350g of vegetables. Garnish with roughly chopped roasted hazelnuts.

## CARROT & CORIANDER

Add 1 heaped teaspoon of ground coriander when cooking the garlic. Only use carrots for the 350g of vegetables. The stalks from a small bunch of fresh coriander can also be added when cooking the carrots and potatoes. When reheating the soup after blending it, add the finely chopped fresh coriander leaves.

## PEA, SMOKED BACON & CRÈME FRAÎCHE

Before cooking the onions, cook 125g of smoked bacon lardons in the fat until crisp, then remove the bacon from the fat with a slotted spoon and keep to one side. Cook the onions in the reserved fat. Use frozen peas and two sticks of diced celery to make up the 350g of vegetables. When reheating the soup after blending it, add the bacon back in. Serve with a dollop of crème fraîche and a few shredded leaves of fresh mint.

# Tomato soup & grilled cheese dippers

If I was American and writing this book, this recipe wouldn't be a modern recipe but rather a traditional one. Its origins in the US date back to the time after World War Two, when grilled cheese sandwiches were added to the school lunch programme and tomato soup was added soon after to boost kids' vitamin C intake. The nostalgia for this combination, along with generations of kids growing up with it in North America, has made it a truly traditional recipe. A relatively new combination here in Ireland, I've no doubt that in years to come Irish kids (and adults) will have the same fondness for it.

Serves 4

1.5kg ripe plum tomatoes, cut into quarters

2 tbsp balsamic vinegar

4 tbsp olive oil

1 tbsp light brown sugar

salt and freshly ground black pepper

2 medium onions, diced

3 garlic cloves, finely chopped

1 carrot, diced

1 celery stick, diced

3 tbsp tomato purée

2 bay leaves

1 litre chicken or vegetable stock

200ml fresh cream, plus extra to garnish (optional)

Preheat the oven to 190°C fan. Line a large baking tray with non-stick baking paper.

In a large bowl, mix the tomatoes with the balsamic vinegar, 2 tablespoons of the olive oil and all of the sugar and season well with salt and pepper. Spread the tomatoes and all the juices out on the prepared baking tray and roast in the preheated oven for 15–20 minutes, until the tomatoes are soft and starting to colour.

Meanwhile, heat the remaining 2 tablespoons of oil in a large saucepan over a medium heat. Add the onions and cook for 5 minutes before adding the garlic and cooking for a further 3 minutes. Add the carrot and celery and cook for 5 minutes more, then add the tomato purée and cook for a further 5 minutes.

Add the roast tomatoes, bay leaves and stock, bring to a simmer and cook for 15–20 minutes, until the vegetables are tender.

While the soup is simmering, make the grilled cheese dippers. Cut the crusts off the slices of bread, then using a rolling pin, flatten each slice a little. Put a slice of cheese on top of each slice of bread and roll it up tightly like a mini Swiss roll. Brush generously with the melted butter and cook in batches in a frying pan over a medium heat until golden all over and the cheese is completely melted. Keep warm in the oven until you're ready to serve.

**To garnish:**

chopped fresh chives

**For the grilled cheese dippers:**

8 slices of white bread

8 slices of processed cheese

50g butter, melted

Using a hand blender, blend the soup till smooth. Add the cream (if using) and heat gently. Season with salt and pepper.

Serve the soup in warm mugs or bowls with an extra drizzle of cream (if using) and a pinch of chopped fresh chives with the grilled cheese dippers on the side.

# Barley broth

What could be more comforting than a bowl of heart-warming broth? It had been years since I had made this and I had forgotten how good this broth makes you feel. It's one of those dishes that makes you feel slightly smug while you're eating it, as it's packed full of flavour, filling, warming and healthy, yet there is a creaminess that comes from slowly cooking the barley that gives it the most incredible richness. During one of the rounds of testing this recipe, I made it completely vegan and was shocked at the level of indulgence that this simple, humble soup gave.

Serves 4 as a soup or 2–3 as a main course

100g pearl barley

1 tbsp vegetable oil

2 medium onions, finely diced

3 garlic cloves, finely chopped

4 small white turnips or 1 small regular turnip/swede, peeled and finely diced

2 medium carrots, finely diced

2 celery stalks, finely diced

1 sprig of fresh thyme or ¼ tsp dried thyme

1 bay leaf

800ml chicken, lamb or vegetable stock

salt and ground white pepper

a small handful of fresh parsley

**To serve:**

crusty bread

Put the barley in a fine mesh sieve and give it a good rinse under a cold running tap to remove any dust.

Heat the oil in a heavy-based saucepan over a medium heat. Add the onions and cook for about 8 minutes, until soft but not coloured, then add the garlic and cook for another 2 minutes. Add the rinsed barley and all the other ingredients except the parsley and season with salt and white pepper. Turn up the heat to bring to a boil, then reduce the heat and simmer for 20 minutes, until the barley and vegetables are tender but still holding their shape.

Add the parsley and check the seasoning – I like lots of white pepper in this broth. Simmer for 5 more minutes.

Serve in warm bowls with some crusty bread on the side for soaking up the broth.

*Note*

If you want to make this soup even more substantial and suitable for a main meal, try adding some boneless, skinless chicken thighs at the beginning of the cooking time. These would need an extra 5 minutes of cooking, so a total cooking time of 25 minutes. Finish with some frozen peas added at the same time as the parsley. Another great version is adding some thinly sliced pieces of lamb – thin enough that they will cook in 25 minutes. I like to finish this version with fresh mint instead of parsley.

# Posh instant noodles

These pimped-up noodles are inspired by two of my favourite noodle dishes: laksa and ramen. I'm not going to claim that simply pouring hot water over a few ingredients is going to give you the same intense flavour that those authentic versions do – rather, I'm using the flavour profiles of a delightful spicy coconut laksa and the deep umami hit of ramen to give a quick and simple lunch a boost. My go-to brand for these simple noodles is Koka, which is available in most Asian shops and supermarkets.

Serves 1

**For the creamy coconut noodles:**

1 x 85g pack of instant noodles (chicken, vegetable or lobster flavours work great)

25g creamed coconut block, grated

¼ yellow pepper, thinly sliced

1 scallion, thinly sliced

1 tsp sriracha sauce

1 tsp fish sauce

a small slice of fresh ginger, peeled and cut into matchsticks

300ml boiling water

**To garnish:**

a few fresh coriander leaves

¼ lime

Using a heatproof lidded container, like a 500g Kilner jar, add all the ingredients except the water and the garnishes in layers, starting with the noodles at the bottom. Be sure to add the contents of the flavour packet from the noodles too.

When you're ready to eat, pour the boiling water over the mixture or until everything is just covered. Close the container and leave for 5 minutes, then give everything a good mix to break up the noodles. Put the lid back on and leave for another 2 minutes. Give it another stir before sprinkling the coriander on top, squeezing the lime juice over and eating immediately.

**For the miso & mushroom noodles:**

1 x 85g pack of instant noodles (beef, mushroom or chicken flavour work great)

50g mushrooms, sliced

25g miso paste

1 soft-boiled egg, halved (see page 11)

½ sheet of nori, cut into strips

1 tsp fish sauce

300ml boiling water

**To garnish:**

1 scallion, thinly sliced

1 tsp toasted sesame seeds

# The best salad sandwich ever!

I know I'm biased but my mum makes the best salad sandwiches ever: finely chopped salad and egg bound with a creamy mayonnaise, packed between two slices of fresh bread spread with a little butter. The only way I've found to improve on her sandwich is to make my own mayonnaise – the little kick of Dijon adds an extra element.

Makes 2

2 hard-boiled eggs
(page 11), finely chopped

2 scallions, finely chopped

2 ripe tomatoes,
quartered, deseeded and
finely diced

1 small head of baby gem,
thinly sliced

¼ cucumber, peeled,
deseeded and finely
chopped

salt and freshly ground
black pepper

4 slices of bread of your
choice

soft butter

**For the mayonnaise:**

2 egg yolks, at room
temperature

1 tbsp Dijon mustard

250ml sunflower oil

2 tsp white wine vinegar

If you want to make your own mayo, put the egg yolks and mustard in a bowl and season with salt and pepper. Using an electric hand mixer, whisk together until combined. Keep the mixer going and add the oil *very* slowly, drop by drop, making sure that the first drop has been incorporated before adding the next drop. Once you can see that the eggs and oil are coming together, you can add a bit more each time. When all the oil has been added, you should have a nice thick mayonnaise. Finally, mix in the vinegar. This will keep in the fridge for three days.

To make the salad filling, simply mix the eggs, scallions, tomatoes, baby gem and cucumber together in a bowl, season with a little salt and pepper and use enough mayonnaise to bind everything together; 2 heaped tablespoons is usually enough.

Butter the four slices of bread. Top two slices with the salad mix, then put the second slice of bread on top.

It may be an Irish thing, but I do like a few crisps on the side – check out page 154 for my homemade salt and vinegar crisps.

# The best Tayto* sandwich ever!

If my mum makes the best salad sandwiches, I definitely make the best crisp sandwiches ever! Not only are we putting a packet of cheese and onion Tayto between two slices of bread, we're also flavouring the bread with not one, not two but three members of the allium family and cheese, not to mention the Tayto going into the bread itself. It might sound like a lot of work but trust me, this bread is a cheese and onion taste explosion.

Makes 1 loaf of bread, enough for lots of Tayto sandwiches

**For the cheese & onion soda bread:**

20g butter, plus extra for greasing

3 tbsp vegetable oil

2 medium onions, thinly sliced

400g plain flour, plus extra for dusting

1 tsp bread soda

1 tsp onion salt

1 small bunch of fresh chives, finely chopped

3 spring onions, thinly sliced

2 bags of Tayto cheese and onion crisps, crushed

80g red Cheddar, grated

350ml buttermilk

1 egg

**To make the sandwiches:**

soft butter

1 bag of Tayto cheese and onion crisps

Heat the butter and 1 tablespoon of the oil in a frying pan over a low heat. Add the onions and cook for 30–40 minutes, stirring occasionally, until they are golden brown and caramelised (yes, it really does take that long to properly caramelise onions!). Remove the pan from the heat and allow the onions to cool completely.

Preheat the oven to 180°C fan. Prepare a 2lb non-stick loaf tin by lightly brushing it with melted butter and dusting with a little plain flour.

Put the flour, bread soda and onion salt in a large bowl and give it a good mix. Add the chives, spring onions, 1½ packets of crisps, the grated cheese and the caramelised onions and mix gently.

Combine the buttermilk, egg and the remaining 2 tablespoons of oil in a jug. Gently whisk together with a fork, then mix into the dry ingredients until it comes together. Add a little more buttermilk if the mixture is too dry – it should be a soft dough.

Transfer the dough into the prepared tin and sprinkle the remaining crisps over the top.

Bake in the preheated oven for 45–50 minutes. To check that the bread is cooked, take it out of the tin and tap the bottom of the bread – it should sound hollow when it's fully cooked. Remove it from the tin and wrap it in a clean tea towel while it's cooling – this will stop the crust from getting too hard.

When the bread is cooled, cut off two slices. Spread each slice with a good layer of soft butter, add a generous layer of cheese and onion Tayto and sandwich together.

*Other brands of crisps are available, of course, but Tayto are the original and, as far as I'm concerned, the best!

# Chicken fillet roll

For years the local deli counters have been creating dishes that have become classic Irish fare, from jambons to breakfast rolls. The chicken fillet roll is even referred to as Irish street food in London.

My brother Pappy works with me in the bakery. He is deaf and non-verbal and loves to go to the local Centra in Stonybatter. I think Pappy gets a kick out of being able to point at his filling, knowing that he's getting what he wants. His choices wouldn't be to my taste, but that's the joy of a deli counter: the combinations are endless. The only tough questions are butter or mayo? Plain, hot or spicy chicken?

Makes 1

20g plain flour

1 tsp garlic powder or granules

1 tsp onion salt

1 tsp paprika

1 tsp dried mixed herbs

½ tsp chilli powder

freshly ground black pepper

1 egg, beaten

50g fresh white breadcrumbs

1 chicken fillet, cut into four even-sized goujons

vegetable oil, for shallow-frying

**For the sandwich:**

1 freshly baked demi baguette

butter or mayo

shredded iceberg

thinly sliced red onion

grated cheese

coleslaw

sliced tomato

taco sauce (see the note)

Put the flour on a wide, shallow plate with the garlic, onion salt, paprika, mixed herbs and chilli powder and mix together – or leave out all the spices if you prefer plain chicken in your chicken fillet roll.

Put the beaten egg in a second bowl and the breadcrumbs in a third bowl.

Working with one goujon at a time, dip it in the seasoned flour, followed by the egg and finally the breadcrumbs, making sure the chicken is completely covered each time. Put the breaded goujon on a plate while you work on the rest. A little tip: when breading food, keep one hand wet and the other hand dry. In other words, use one hand to pick up the chicken and take it out of the egg and use the other hand to take it from the flour and breadcrumbs.

Heat a good layer of oil in a small frying pan over a medium heat – you want to shallow-fry the chicken. Add the breaded goujons and cook for 6–8 minutes on each side, until golden brown and cooked through.

To make the sandwich, split the baguette in half lengthways. Spread the top and bottom with butter or mayo or any other sauce you like (see the note if, like Pappy, you like taco sauce on your roll). Add the chicken goujons or slices and whatever other fillings you like.

## Note

If you're like Pappy and like taco sauce on your chicken fillet roll, make your own by mixing 3 tablespoons mayo with 1 tablespoon tomato sauce, ½ teaspoon chilli powder, ½ teaspoon garlic powder and a pinch of ground cumin.

# Variations

## GREAT IN BREAD

There is nothing more convenient than sticking something tasty between two slices of bread or in a roll. From the now-famous breakfast roll to the more retro sugar sandwich, Ireland has always loved filling bread as a form of nourishment.

### CHEAT'S PRAWN COCKTAIL SANDWICH

I love a crisp sandwich and I love experimenting by putting different crisps in my sandwiches. During a conversation with my friend Ali Dunworth backstage at a festival where she had created a DIY crisp sandwich station, I had the idea for a scampi fries sandwich: sliced fresh white bread with Marie Rose sauce, iceberg lettuce, and whole and broken scampi fries. It is pure perfection, trust me!

### BANANA SANDWICH

This is a favourite from my childhood, when my mum would mash bananas with a little whipped cream and a sprinkling of sugar as a filling in a sandwich of fresh white bread. It was so good. When I fancy a banana sandwich nowadays, it's usually sliced banana with some smoked streaky bacon and a little peanut butter.

### HANG SANDWICH

You can't beat two slices of fresh white sliced pan with a generous spread of butter, lots of good-quality 'hang' (ham) and a side of brown sauce or mustard for smearing.

# Bánh mì

Over Christmas and New Year of 2017 into 2018, my husband, Daithí, and I were lucky enough to do a bit of travelling around Vietnam, Cambodia and Thailand. I had done my research before we went and knew that I had a few things I needed to check off my taste list (it's like a bucket list but for food): I wanted to try egg coffee and pho in Vietnam, amok in Cambodia and all the curries in Thailand.

What I wasn't expecting to be totally blown away by, though, was the bánh mì in Vietnam. There was one in particular that I can still remember, from a little food stand by the entrance to our hotel in Ho Chi Minh City. One day we were heading to the Mekong Delta and I decided to grab two for the bus journey. Light, fluffy bread; pâté; pickled daikon and carrot; fresh coriander; roast pork belly; fried quail eggs; mayonnaise; and a spicy tomato sauce. I don't remember much of the Mekong Delta, but I do remember that sandwich.

Makes 2

**For the pork belly:**

150g pork belly, cut into thick slices

1 garlic clove, finely chopped

1 tsp soy sauce

1 tsp honey

**For the easy pickles:**

2 tbsp white wine vinegar

1 tsp honey

¼ tsp salt

1 small carrot, peeled and cut into ribbons using the peeler

4 radishes, cut as thinly as possible

Start by marinating the pork belly strips in the garlic, soy and honey for 1 hour.

Meanwhile, make the simple pickle by whisking the vinegar, honey and salt together in a bowl. Add the carrot ribbons and radishes and give them a good stir to coat with the dressing.

Set your grill to its highest setting.

Put the pork belly on a grilling rack and grill for about 15 minutes, turning the strips over halfway through. You want the pork to be crisp and caramelised.

To make the sandwiches, split each bread roll lengthways. Spread the bottom half with pâté (if using) and mayonnaise on the top. If you aren't using the pâté, spread a layer of mayonnaise on the bottom as well. Divide the crispy pork belly strips between the two bottom halves and top with the pickles, lots of fresh coriander leaves and two fried quail eggs (if using). Drizzle over a little sriracha, sandwich together with the top half of the bread and serve.

**For the sandwiches:**

2 large bread rolls – you want something light and fluffy, not too crusty

2 tbsp pâté (optional)

mayonnaise (homemade on page 64 or shop-bought)

1 small bunch of fresh coriander, leaves picked

4 fried quail eggs (optional)

a drizzle of sriracha sauce

# Pork & Bacon

# GROWING UP AT
# Number·4

Food has always been a part of my life. I lived above my family's pork and bacon butcher shop at 4 Duke Street in Athy, Kildare until I was 18 years old. When I reminisce about growing up above the shop, my senses transport me back to that special place. The smell of the spices and seasoning that were used for sausages or dusted onto pork chops that were rich in nutmeg and would tickle the inside of your nose if inhaled too deeply. The sounds of the hand-cranked bacon slicer as it swooshed back and forth, the voices of customers placing their orders. The sight of the shop window decorated with swags of sausages and adorned with rings of black and white pudding and red baloney. The cool touch of the terrazzo counter or the warm, velvet-like feeling of the freshly scrubbed butchers' block. But what sticks out most in my memory are the tastes: warm crubeens, freshly cooked ham, roast pork, sausages. All the pork and bacon goodness.

# Sticky fingers and jelly-smacked lips

**BY KATE RYAN**

IT'S SATURDAY, THE DAY FOR COOKING HAM HOCKS AND CRUBEENS IN GIANT BOILERS HOUSED IN THE YARD BEHIND HERTERICH'S BUTCHER SHOP IN ATHY TOWN CENTRE. CUSTOMERS WILL SOON ARRIVE TO COLLECT THEIR PRE-ORDERED HOCKS AND TROTTERS ALONG WITH HERTERICH'S FAMOUS SAUSAGES, PUDDINGS, BACON, HAMS AND FRESHLY ROASTED PORK.

Bobby Mahon, Graham's uncle, delivers up these still-hot gelatinous treats in a large pail, setting it down against a wall in a small hallway that separates the butchers' shop downstairs from the family home upstairs. Wise to Uncle Bobby's routine and patiently waiting for him to retreat to the yard, Graham and his brother, Pappy, cheekily hunt out any low-hanging porky fruit – a little feather of hock here, a glutinous devourment of crubeen there.

Beware of quiet children, for it undoubtedly means mischief is afoot – in Graham and Pappy's case, quite literally a foot. Eventually, someone – Graham's father, Paul, his mother, Ann, or Bobby maybe – will uncover the duo, all glued up with sticky fingers and jelly-smacked lips and seen off from the bucket of goodies.

Would Mrs Murphy get the six trotters she asked for or just four today? Well, a six-legged pig is fierce difficult to catch, after all …

\*\*\*

Graham's grandfather, Ernie, began trading as Herterich's Butchers on Duke Street, Athy, County Kildare in February 1942. Ernie died young at 53 from a brain tumour in 1967. His son, Paul (Graham's father), apprenticed under his father from age 16 after leaving school but had barely two years working alongside him until his untimely death. Ernie left a lasting impression on Paul and, by extension, Graham: 'He wasn't God, but he was God to me,' says Paul.

During Herterich's heyday, Athy was a bustling market town with 11 butcher shops. Most were victuallers of beef and lamb; only Herterich's specialised in pork and bacon. The family, as the uniqueness of the name suggests, came to Ireland via Bavaria, Germany, and it's true to say that anyone who bears the name Herterich in Ireland today is a branch off this original wind-blown tree.

Herterich's was embedded in the community and three generations of the family lived over the shop. Over the years, until the doors closed for the final time in 1997, the shop fed the people of Athy many thousands of times over, and both Paul and Ernie prided themselves on never seeing anyone go without. If someone asked for six chops instead of enough to feed the 10 mouths known to be at home, in would go what was needed. Nobody was left wanting for anything, and nothing went to waste – even the dogs of Athy were well fed on scraps of ham and roast pork left on the slicer.

Ernie Herterich's week began with travelling to houses and cottages in Athy, collecting pigs booked in for slaughter that week. It was typical back then for every butcher to operate their own abattoir, and when all the pigs had been rounded up and brought back to Herterich's, Bobby was ready to enact their dispatch.

'Back then, people used pigs as a kind of bank,' says Paul. 'They might have kids going for communion or confirmation, so the idea for keeping a pig was that it'd pay for everything.' The original piggy banks!

Saturday, the shop would be full to bursting with a queue snaking patiently along the street.

'At the time you wouldn't have a supermarket selling sausages and rashers, so if you wanted that, you had to come to Herterich's. On a Saturday morning, there would be a queue going out the door with people waiting to come in,' says Paul.

Busy mothers sent their children down to hold a place in the queue while they got on with other necessities. A family friend was often sent down to stand in the Herterich queue for the bones of an hour, and only when he reached the top of the queue would his mother follow on down.

## 'The shop was our home, and the shop was my dad,' says Graham. 'The shop was everything to him, and that has influenced who I am and who I want to be in food.'

Bobby spent much of his time in the yard corralling pigs, preparing puddings and sausages, and boiling the hocks, crubeens, offal and pigs' heads for making brawn and hazlet. He is remembered as a hardy, strong man yet with a delicate touch to his labour; a master of puddings with agile hands able to manoeuvre the still-steaming puddings from the boiler.

'He'd have the twine in his mouth wrapping it around making the puddings, tying them off as quick as anything,' says Paul.

While the yard was the coalface of production, most of the butchery happened in the shop, which, by contrast, was bright and modern, with dazzling polished terrazzo floors that seamlessly merged into the sleek counters with their elegant displays of handcrafted victuals.

A bustling hustle of customers could easily fit inside on any day, but on the 'big days' of Friday and

Signature meats, like boiled hams, roast pork and bacon rashers, sat ready and primed, pre-sliced and weighed out into packs of quarter and half pounds with greaseproof paper in between. There were always 16 sausages in a pound, too, invariably just over the pound but never under.

Sausages were a speciality of Herterich's for two reasons: the meat was all chopped by hand to Ernie's exacting standards and never minced, a technique Paul refers to as 'the chopping' brought over from Germany, where a coarser texture is preferred, and for its unique seasoning.

'Every Thursday, my father travelled to Dublin and visited William Blake's to pick up casings and all the seasonings. He'd get a newspaper, the old broadsheets, fold it in two, cut it into a square, put that on the scale and weigh off the salt and white pepper. He'd a row of tins under the counter – sage, coriander, nutmeg, paprika – and he'd have a fistful of that one but only a pinch of that one. You'd look along the counter and here were all these colours, the reds, yellows, white – I always remember that – the colours along the counter of all the different seasonings. Then he'd mix it all together and fold the packet in a certain way. That was his seasoning for the chopping, and he'd place it on the shelf underneath the counter.'

Ernie passed away without sharing the formula for his secret seasoning. Paul got it close, but he admits, 'They never got it dead right!'

This association with spice is three generations deep and engrained in Graham's sensory memory.

'We had a small fridge. I never remember it working; it was only ever used as the spice store,' Graham says. 'The smell of the spices lingered in there, like it was embedded. It sounds funny, but I can still smell that warm spicing smell even now, that heavy hit of nutmeg.'

Imagine swags of sausages coloured red and white, black puddings, whole sides of bacon, cooked ham coated with a bright yellow crumb, and meats displayed neatly interspersed with old-fashioned green and red edging. Then stepping into the shining terrazzo shop buzzing with customers and a crew of white-coated happy and familiar Herterich staff waiting to serve you. A festive visit to Herterich's was quite the spectacle.

There was a little Christmas tree in a small room behind the shop with a window just big enough to spy its glinting lights and adornment of chocolates. Every child was invited to choose a favoured one and the tree stayed resplendently abundant with festive treats until it was taken down on 14 January, after Paul's birthday – a Herterich family tradition.

Once the last customer was served and the door closed on Christmas Eve, whatever was left over was carefully packed into parcels and taken to those in need of a helping hand.

## As far as Herterich family traditions go, their instinct for generosity and an almost compulsive quality to share in the joy that food can bring is surely the best one of all.

That scent of warming spices is redolent and heady with the prospect of Christmastime, the busiest time of all for the Herterich family. At Christmas, but also for Easter and St Patrick's Day, as though to emphasise the feasting element of this trinity of Irish festival days, the window display of Herterich's butcher shop was something wondrous to behold.

'We'd have many hams and legs of pork, and sausages, thick and thin, were hung in the window right along,' says Paul. 'Some of the sausages we would colour bright red with polony dye. There'd be a ham coming down and hanging in between, and at each end two sides of back bacon. Underneath would be all the different cuts of meat.'

'The shop was our home, and the shop was my dad,' says Graham. 'The shop was everything to him, and that has influenced who I am and who I want to be in food. But it's more than that. It's the way Dad interacted with and treated customers and all the people in the shop; the way he dealt with people. If someone was short a bob or two, they wouldn't leave the shop without.'

As far as Herterich family traditions go, their instinct for generosity and an almost compulsive quality to share in the joy that food can bring is surely the best one of all.

# Bacon & cabbage

It's funny how a plate of food can be so thought provoking that it constantly reminds you of a time in your life. Because my dad was a pork and bacon butcher, this is one of those dishes that we had quite regularly when I was growing up, but it will always remind me of 7up – specifically, green 7up. You see, on St Patrick's Day, Mum would always add a few drops of green food colouring into 7up as a once-a-year treat for our special meal, which as far as I can remember was bacon and cabbage most years. It's still one of my favourites to this day.

Serves 4–6

1.5kg loin of bacon

1 small onion, peeled and cut in half

1 carrot, cut in half widthways

2 celery sticks, cut in half widthways

1 bay leaf

1 tsp black peppercorns

1 large head of cabbage

25g butter

salt and freshly ground black pepper

**To serve:**

parsley sauce (page 11)

boiled or mashed potatoes (page 13)

Put the bacon in a large saucepan, cover it with cold water and bring to a boil. When it comes to a boil, discard the water and fill the saucepan again with cold water. Add the onion, carrot, celery, bay leaf and peppercorns. Bring to a boil again, then reduce the heat to a simmer and cook the bacon for 20 minutes per 500g (a 1.5kg loin of bacon will take 1 hour to cook).

While the bacon is cooking, prepare the cabbage by thinly slicing it, removing any tough stalks and the core. You can also take this time to make the parsley sauce as per the recipe on page 11.

Remove the bacon from the water when it's cooked and set aside to rest. Use a slotted spoon or small sieve to remove the vegetables, bay leaf and peppercorns from the water. Bring the water back to a boil, then add the cabbage. Cook for 5–10 minutes – this will depend on the type of cabbage (see page 85). When cooked, drain the cabbage well, return it to the pot and add the butter. Toss together and check for seasoning.

Carve the bacon into slices and serve with the buttered cabbage, parsley sauce and boiled or mashed potatoes on the side.

## Note

You can make this into a bacon and cabbage filo pie – see the recipe on page 132.

# Variations

## BAGÚN, CABÁISTE AGUS PEIRSIL

### TYPES OF BACON

**Collar of bacon:** Cut from the central muscle of the shoulder. A seam of fat runs through the bacon that adds flavour and moisture during cooking.

**Back/loin of bacon:** A premium cut of meat taken from the back. This is the cured version of where pork chops would be taken from and where back rashers come from.

**Bacon belly:** Quite a fatty cut of bacon but it has so much flavour. This is where streaky rashers come from.

## TYPES OF CABBAGE

**Savoy cabbage:** Keep an eye out for the January King variety, with its pale-green interior and deep purple and green leaves on the outside. This one is my favourite.

**York/pointed cabbage:** A lighter cabbage with a milder but sometimes more peppery flavour. My favourites are sweetheart or Hispi. Hispi cabbage has become trendy in recent years, with many chefs and restaurants using it on their menus – see the next page for my version.

**Green cabbage:** A tightly packed head of cabbage with a mild peppery flavour that lessens when cooked.

**Dutch/red cabbage:** These are not suitable for bacon and cabbage but work well in coleslaw and are also suitable for roasting and braising.

## TYPES OF PARSLEY

**Curly:** This was the only type of parsley I ever saw before the early 2000s. It's packed full of flavour and is still my go-to.

**Flat-leaf:** Probably more readily available these days and is easier to clean but I feel it lacks a little in flavour compared to curly parsley. However, it's a better choice for those dishes where you want the parsley to be roughly chopped.

# Cabbage & bacon

The flavour you get from roasting cabbage is unbelievable. The outside char has a nutty flavour, while the inside steams during the cooking to bring out the most incredible sweet flavour. Pair the cabbage with smoked bacon, butter-fried breadcrumbs, a crunch of hazelnuts and a caramelised onion sauce and you won't be sorry. This dish celebrates a humble ingredient and makes it the star.

Serves 2 as a main or 4 as a side dish

2 tbsp duck fat or vegetable oil

1 Hispi cabbage, outer leaves removed and discarded, then cut into quarters

125g smoked bacon lardons

2 garlic cloves, finely chopped

100g fresh white breadcrumbs

50g butter

50g hazelnuts, roughly chopped

a small handful of fresh parsley, finely chopped

1 batch of soubise sauce (page 11)

Preheat the oven to 160°C fan.

Heat the duck fat or vegetable oil in an ovenproof frying pan over a medium-high heat. Add the cabbage to the pan, cut sides down, and brown each wedge on both of its cut sides until each side has taken on a deep golden colour. Turn the wedges cut side up, transfer the pan to the preheated oven and cook for 15–20 minutes, until they are tender. The best way to test this is to pierce each wedge with a knife – it should glide in easily.

Meanwhile, cook the bacon lardons in a frying pan over a medium-high heat, stirring occasionally, until cooked through and crisp. Add the garlic and cook for another minute, then add the breadcrumbs, butter and hazelnuts and continue to cook for a further 4–5 minutes, stirring continuously, until the breadcrumbs are golden and crisp. Stir in the parsley.

To serve, spread the soubise sauce on a serving plate, top with the cabbage wedges and scatter over the crumb topping.

# Bangers & mash

There are two types of people in the world: those who like their bangers (sausages) and mash with onion gravy and those who like it with beans. I am very much the latter but I also like it with a fried egg. That magical mound of mash with beans in its crater and capped with a runny fried egg is heaven!

So why am I giving you onion gravy? Because it reminds me of another dinner we had growing up. Mum used to make beef burgers and finish cooking them in an onion gravy. Feel free to swap the sausages in this recipe for beef burgers – the only difference is that instead of serving the onion gravy on the side, put the pan-fried burgers in a baking dish, pour over the gravy and finish cooking the burgers in the oven for about 15 minutes.

Serves 4

1 tbsp vegetable oil

8–12 best-quality pork sausages, depending on size

**For the onion gravy:**

20g butter

3 medium onions, thinly sliced

1 tsp light brown sugar

a pinch of dried thyme

1 tbsp balsamic vinegar

25g plain flour

400ml beef stock

**To serve:**

mashed potatoes (page 13)

Preheat the oven to 120°C fan.

Heat the oil in a frying pan over a medium-high heat. Add the sausages and cook for 10–12 minutes, turning occasionally, until golden all over and cooked through. Transfer to a plate and keep warm in the oven while you make the gravy.

Add the butter to any residual fat that's left in the frying pan, then add the onions, sugar and thyme. Cook for 10–15 minutes, until the onions have taken on a deep golden colour and are slightly caramelised. Add the vinegar and let it almost evaporate before stirring in the flour. Stir in the beef stock and bring to a boil, then reduce the heat and simmer for 3–4 minutes. Decant the gravy into a jug.

Bring everything to the table to serve family style: mounds of mash topped with a few sausages and a generous pouring of onion gravy.

# Meatballs & polenta

There is something so comforting about meatballs, and I'm not just talking about the type of meatballs in this recipe. I'm lucky to have eaten meatballs in several different countries, from bowls of noodle soup with chewy meatballs in Vietnam called phô bò viên to lamb mince and liver wrapped in caul called skilpadjies in South Africa and beef ktzitzot in Jerusalem. I have yet to get to Sweden, but like many, many people I have eaten köttbullar with creamy gravy and lingonberry jam – yes, IKEA meatballs! There are other meatballs I've added to my bucket list, like keftedes in Greece, albóndigas in Spain and pulpety in Poland. The world is your oyster meatball – go enjoy them!

Serves 4

3 tbsp olive oil

1 medium onion, finely chopped

4 garlic cloves, finely chopped

300g beef mince

300g pork mince (or you can use all beef mince if you prefer)

50g fresh white breadcrumbs

1 tsp dried oregano

2 tsp Dijon mustard

1 medium egg, beaten

salt and freshly ground black pepper

1 ball of fresh mozzarella, cut into 16 pieces (optional)

Heat 2 tablespoons of the oil in a frying pan over a medium heat. Add the onion and cook gently for about 5 minutes, until starting to soften. Add the garlic and cook for a further 2 minutes, then put half of the onion and garlic mixture in a large bowl and the other half in a small bowl. Allow both to cool completely.

Put the mince, breadcrumbs, oregano, mustard and egg in the large mixing bowl on top of the cooled onion and garlic. Season generously with salt and freshly ground black pepper. With clean hands, mix everything together well.

Divide this meat mixture into quarters, then divide each quarter into quarters yet again to get 16 portions. Using wet hands, roll each portion into a ball. If you're using the mozzarella, make a deep indent in the centre of each ball with your finger, put a piece of cheese in the indent and roll it again to ensure the cheese is completely enclosed. When all 16 meatballs have been made, put them on a large plate, cover with cling film and chill in the fridge for at least half an hour to allow them to firm up before frying. These can be made up to 24 hours beforehand.

Heat the remaining tablespoon of oil in a large frying pan over a medium-high heat. Add the meatballs in batches and cook until they are brown on all sides. Transfer to a plate and set aside. ⊕

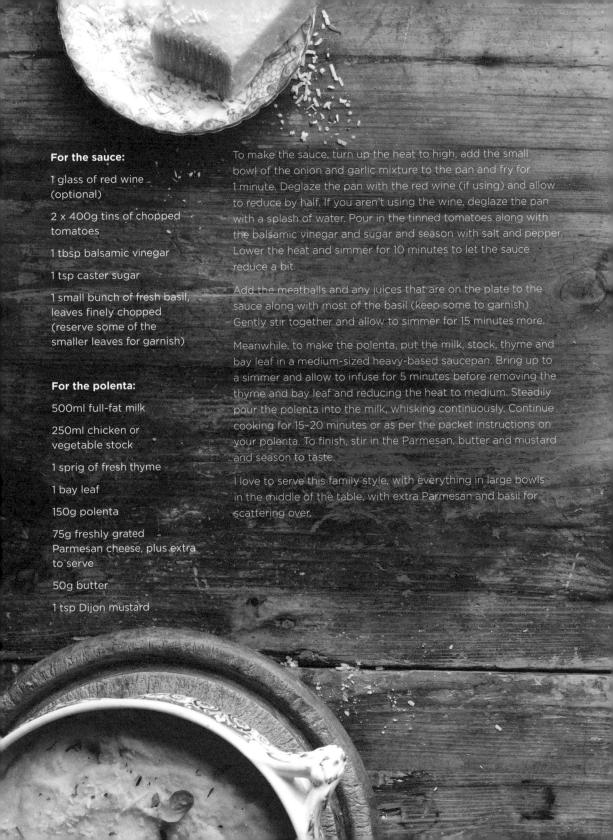

### For the sauce:

1 glass of red wine (optional)

2 x 400g tins of chopped tomatoes

1 tbsp balsamic vinegar

1 tsp caster sugar

1 small bunch of fresh basil, leaves finely chopped (reserve some of the smaller leaves for garnish)

### For the polenta:

500ml full-fat milk

250ml chicken or vegetable stock

1 sprig of fresh thyme

1 bay leaf

150g polenta

75g freshly grated Parmesan cheese, plus extra to serve

50g butter

1 tsp Dijon mustard

To make the sauce, turn up the heat to high, add the small bowl of the onion and garlic mixture to the pan and fry for 1 minute. Deglaze the pan with the red wine (if using) and allow to reduce by half. If you aren't using the wine, deglaze the pan with a splash of water. Pour in the tinned tomatoes along with the balsamic vinegar and sugar and season with salt and pepper. Lower the heat and simmer for 10 minutes to let the sauce reduce a bit.

Add the meatballs and any juices that are on the plate to the sauce along with most of the basil (keep some to garnish). Gently stir together and allow to simmer for 15 minutes more.

Meanwhile, to make the polenta, put the milk, stock, thyme and bay leaf in a medium-sized heavy-based saucepan. Bring up to a simmer and allow to infuse for 5 minutes before removing the thyme and bay leaf and reducing the heat to medium. Steadily pour the polenta into the milk, whisking continuously. Continue cooking for 15–20 minutes or as per the packet instructions on your polenta. To finish, stir in the Parmesan, butter and mustard and season to taste.

I love to serve this family style, with everything in large bowls in the middle of the table, with extra Parmesan and basil for scattering over.

# Bridie McGrath's coddle

Coddle is a Dublin dish that's rooted in tradition – each family has their own recipe for it. I'm a Kildare man, so I'm never going to write a recipe for coddle – I'll leave that to my friend Noel, who is from East Wall in Dublin and was taught to cook coddle by his mam, Bridie. Noel says, 'Coddle is one of the foods I always remember my mam making on a regular basis. The smell alone brings me back to sitting at the table in front of a white pudding bowl filled to the brim with coddle, with a side plate of buttered white bread to mop up the remnants. I must have watched her prepare it so many times, but it was only when I finally left home that I managed to get the recipe and the chance to cook it. Only Mother was allowed to cook in her kitchen for fear that anyone else would make a mess. One of the first meals I cooked for Mam and Dad in my own home was coddle and it felt like giving something special back to them. I have since cooked it for a lot of my friends of many different nationalities, including in the middle of summer in Sydney.

'There are as many variations of coddle as there are mothers in Dublin. This is my mam's version and the one I still love to this day. Some people can be put off by the sausages being boiled, but I was never tempted to brown them first. It's just one of those put-everything-in-the-pot-and-let-it-go kind of dishes. It's simple and requires very little effort, yet you are rewarded with a tasty, warming meal. My brother had his own interesting version. It was green (from some peas) and had burgers floating in it – not one I'd recommend trying, even as a modern twist.'

Serves 4

675g floury potatoes (see page 14), peeled and cut into large chunks or quarters

1 medium onion, peeled and cut into 8 wedges

8 pork sausages

300g bacon pieces (see the note)

100g red lentils

1 tsp Saxa ground black or white pepper (add more if you like)

1 litre water

**To serve:**

buttered bread

Layer the ingredients in a heavy-based pot in the following order: potatoes, onion, sausages, bacon, lentils. Season with the ground black or white pepper, then pour over the water until it just covers the ingredients – it should be about 1 litre. Cover the pot with a lid and bring to a boil on a high heat, then reduce the heat and simmer with the lid slightly ajar. Cook for 30 minutes, until the potatoes start to break down and the lentils have disappeared and have thickened the sauce.

To serve, divide among warm bowls with buttered bread on the side for mopping up the broth.

# Chorizo & butternut stew

Have you ever noticed that sometimes food can have the most unusual descriptions? It might be that a chilli is as hot as hell or a strawberry tastes like a summer day. I say this because I think that this dish is bursting with sunshine! It's slightly spicy from the heat from the chorizo, a little smoky from the bacon, packed with flavour from the onion, garlic and tomatoes, and all with the slightly sweet taste of the butternut squash.

## Serves 4

200g dry-cured chorizo, cut into bite-sized chunks

125g smoked bacon lardons

1 medium onion, sliced

1 tbsp olive oil (if needed)

3 garlic cloves, finely chopped

2 x 400g tins of chopped tomatoes

1 medium butternut squash, peeled and cut into 5cm chunks

1 tsp dried oregano

½ tsp smoked paprika

1 tsp dried chilli flakes

1 tsp caster sugar

salt and freshly ground black pepper

1 small bunch of fresh flat-leaf parsley, roughly chopped

**To serve:**

sour cream

crusty white bread

Put the chorizo and smoked bacon lardons in a cold, dry, deep frying pan and put the pan on a medium-high heat. The slow increase in temperature will help the chorizo to release its red oil. Once the chorizo and bacon start frying, cook for about 3 minutes. Use a slotted spoon to remove the chorizo and bacon and set them aside on a plate, leaving all the fat that has rendered out in the pan.

Add the onion to the pan and cook it in the red oil for about 5 minutes, until starting to soften. Depending on how much oil the chorizo has released, you may need to add 1 tablespoon of olive oil to help the onion cook. Add the garlic and cook for a further 2 minutes.

Add the tinned tomatoes, then add a splash of water to each empty tin, swirling it around to remove any tomato still clinging to the sides and add that to the pan too. Add the squash, oregano, smoked paprika and chilli flakes. Add the chorizo and bacon back to the pan. Give everything a good stir and bring to a boil, then reduce the heat to a low simmer and cook for 20–25 minutes, until the squash has softened. Add a dash of water during the cooking if it starts to look a little dry.

When cooked, add the sugar and season to taste with salt and pepper, then stir through most of the parsley. I like to serve this in warm bowls with a dollop of sour cream and the remaining parsley scattered on top and lots of crusty white bread on the side.

# Hazlet

In our butcher shop, all the different cooked meats were made in-house by my dad and the other butchers: two different types of ham (whole and pressed), roast pork with a layer of crackling and its beautiful marbling, a pressed terrine of cheek and tongue, the vibrant red brawn and finally, my favourite: hazlet, a pork meatloaf flavoured with lots of sage, onion and pepper that's served cold and cut into slices.

## Makes 1 loaf (8–10 portions)

25g butter, plus extra for greasing and for melting over the top

1 large onion, finely chopped

500g pork mince

100g fresh white breadcrumbs

25–50g pork liver, finely chopped (optional)

1 egg, beaten

150ml milk

1 small bunch of fresh parsley, finely chopped

3 tbsp finely chopped fresh sage or 1 tbsp dried sage

1 tsp salt

½ tsp ground white pepper

¼ tsp ground black pepper

Preheat the oven to 180°C fan. Grease a 2lb loaf tin with butter.

Melt the butter in a frying pan over a medium heat. When the butter is foaming, add the onion and cook for 10 minutes, until softened and golden. Remove the pan from the heat and allow to cool completely.

Put all the remaining ingredients in a large mixing bowl, including the cooled onion, and use clean hands to mix everything together thoroughly. If you would like a finer texture to your hazlet, blend everything together in a food processor instead.

Fill the greased tin with the mixture, making sure it's tightly packed and that there are no air pockets. Traditionally there would be a slight dome to the hazlet. Brush the top with a little melted butter.

Boil your kettle and put the filled tin in a deep roasting tray. Transfer the tray to the preheated oven, then pull the oven shelf out slightly. Pour the boiling water into the roasting tray until it comes halfway up the sides of the tin to create a bain-marie.

Cook in the oven for 1 hour, until the juices run clear when a skewer is inserted into the middle of the loaf. Allow to cool for 15 minutes before taking the loaf out of the tin and transferring it to a board. Allow to cool completely.

Serve cold, cut into thin slices with buttered bread, pickles and mustard on the side. This also works well cut into slices and served hot, straight from the oven, or allowed to cool, then cut into thick slices and fried in a little butter.

# Pork rillettes

Looking back on growing up in and over the family butcher shop, I now realise how skilled my father and the other butchers were. They weren't only craft butchers, they were skilled producers of charcuterie, a word that was relatively unknown in Ireland in the 1980s. To everyone who visited our shop, these men simply made damn good cooked meats.

Pork rillettes are some of the first charcuterie I ever remember making. It does take a little bit of time, but trust me, it's time well spent. Share it as a starter or as part of a bigger grazing board or have it for lunches and snacks throughout the week.

Serves 8

1kg rindless and boneless pork belly, cut into 5cm pieces

2 shallots, thinly sliced

6 garlic cloves, grated

1 large shot of brandy

2 sprigs of fresh thyme

2 bay leaves, plus extra to garnish

2 whole star anise, plus extra to garnish

12 juniper berries, crushed and roughly chopped, plus extra to garnish

salt and freshly ground black pepper

250ml water

4 tbsp duck fat, melted (optional)

**To serve:**

toasted sourdough

pickled vegetables (page 72)

Tip all the ingredients except the water and duck fat into a large bowl and season generously. Give everything a good mix, cover the bowl with cling film and marinate in the fridge overnight.

The next day, preheat the oven to 120°C fan.

Transfer the mixture to a large heavy-based casserole that's suitable for the hob and add the water. Put on a medium heat and as soon as it starts bubbling, cover the casserole with its lid, transfer to the preheated oven and cook for 2–3 hours, until the meat is very tender.

Remove from the oven and allow to cool slightly. Drain the meat over a bowl to catch all the fat and liquid. Pick out the thyme and bay leaves and, if possible, the juniper berries. Using two forks, shred the meat, being careful not to overwork the meat to a paste. Taste the meat and add extra seasoning if required.

Press the meat into eight individual ramekins or one large baking dish. Pour the juices and fat back over the meat and put in the fridge to set for at least 2 hours.

If you would like to preserve the rillette for a little longer, cover the top with melted duck fat and garnish with extra bay leaves, juniper berries and star anise.

Serve with crusty bread and pickles on the side to cut through the richness.

# Roast pork belly

Pork and apple are such good friends that's it's hard for any other fruit to get a look in! But there are a few other fruits that work well with the sweet, fatty taste of pork, in particular soft stone fruits like plums, apricots and peaches as well as pineapple, pear and in this case, rhubarb. I like to serve this as part of a weekend roast, but it would work just as well with a selection of salads for a more casual lunch.

Serves 4–6

2 star anise

1 tbsp coriander seeds

½ tsp chilli flakes

40g flaky sea salt

½ tsp ground white pepper

1.5kg boneless pork belly

**For the roast rhubarb compote:**

300g rhubarb, cut into 5cm pieces

zest and juice of 1 orange

1½ tbsp caster sugar

25g butter, cut into small pieces

**To serve:**

celeriac, brown butter and pear mash (page 144)

Using a spice grinder or a pestle and mortar, crush the star anise, coriander seeds and chilli flakes together. Stir in the salt and pepper.

The night before you want to serve this, put the pork belly, skin side up, in a dish that you can put in the fridge. Using a sharp knife, score lines in the pork skin about 5mm apart. Rub three-quarters of the salt and spice mixture into the pork skin, making sure you get it into the cuts. Save the rest of the mixture in an airtight container for the next day. Put the pork in the fridge overnight, uncovered.

The following day, preheat the oven to 150°C fan.

Remove the pork from the fridge and scrape the salt off the skin. Use kitchen paper to dry the pork as much as possible. Season all over with the remaining salt mixture and put in a roasting tray.

Roast the pork in the preheated oven for 2 hours, then reduce the temperature to 130°C fan and cook for 1 hour more. Finally, turn up the temperature of the oven as high as it will go and cook for another 15 minutes, until the skin has a nice crackling. Remove from the oven and allow to rest for half an hour.

When the pork has been removed from the oven, reduce the heat to 180°C fan. Line a baking tray with non-stick baking paper.

Mix the rhubarb, orange zest and juice and the sugar together. Spread the rhubarb and all the juices out on the lined tray, then scatter the butter across the top. Roast in the oven for 15–20 minutes, until the rhubarb is starting to fall apart. Pour the rhubarb and all the juices in a small saucepan and stir to break down the rhubarb.

To serve, cut the pork belly into thick slices and add the warm roast rhubarb compote and the celeriac, brown butter and pear mash alongside.

# Marmalade pork belly
## with cabbage & orange salad

I love how loyal we are to our own brands here in Ireland with the likes of Lyons, Avonmore, Jacob's, Brennans, Kerrygold, Barry's and Batchelors. I have gone to another iconic Irish brand for this recipe: Old Time Irish Marmalade, the one with the cat sitting in front of an open fire on the label. Made originally by Lamb's Jams with a history going back to the 1850s, the coarsely cut marmalade is a real taste of Ireland. The combination of the pork with the hit of ginger and garlic along with the sticky orange marmalade just works.

Serves 4

100g Old Time Irish Marmalade

2 garlic cloves, finely chopped

2.5cm piece of ginger, peeled and grated

1 tbsp white wine vinegar

1 tbsp vegetable oil

500g pork belly strips

**For the cabbage & orange salad:**

50ml olive oil

juice of 1 lemon

2 heaped tbsp Old Time Irish Marmalade

1 tbsp Dijon mustard

2 large oranges

1 Chinese/napa cabbage, shredded

5 spring onions, thinly sliced at an angle

a handful of radishes, thinly sliced

In a roasting dish that isn't so big that the pork is lost in it, add the marmalade, garlic, ginger, vinegar and oil and mash them together with a fork. Add the pork and cover each piece with a layer of the marinade. Cover with cling film and marinate for a few hours in the fridge.

Preheat the oven to 140°C fan.

Remove the cling film from the dish and cover it tightly with a sheet of foil. Cook in the preheated oven for 2–2½ hours, until the meat is completely tender.

In the meantime, make the salad by putting the olive oil, lemon juice, marmalade and mustard in a large bowl and whisking it together for a minute until you have a thick dressing.

Use a shape knife to peel the oranges, doing your best to remove the white pith. Now cut each orange in half from top to bottom, then cut each half into slices, cutting across the orange. Add the oranges and any of their juices to the dressing along with the cabbage, scallions and radishes. Give everything a good mix and keep chilled.

To finish the pork belly, heat the grill to its highest setting. If the pork belly has released a lot of water, pour the juices and marinade into a small saucepan and reduce for a few minutes over a high heat. Put the belly on a suitable baking tray and brush with some of this sauce. Grill for 4–5 minutes on each side, brushing with the sauce several times, until the pork is stick and slightly charred. (You could also do this final stage on a barbecue.)

Serve the pork with the fresh salad on the side.

# Dinner

# Savoury mince

Savoury mince with hot potatoes brings me back to happy times and adventures with Aiden Prendergast (or Ned, as we affectionately called him) and all the 5th Kildare Scouts. It was one of the go-to meals for camps in places like Larch Hill and Lough Dan and it's what we would cook for competitions like the regional Shield and the all-Ireland Melvin. That is, until I became quartermaster and cook for the Hawk Patrol and convinced my mum to teach me how to make beef stroganoff, but I digress.

Serves 4

2 tbsp vegetable oil

1 medium onion, finely diced

2 garlic cloves, finely chopped

500g beef mince

2 carrots, finely diced

1 celery stick, finely diced

2 tbsp tomato purée

1 tbsp plain flour

400ml beef stock

a good splash of Worcestershire sauce

2 bay leaves

1 tsp dried mixed herbs

salt and freshly ground black pepper

100g frozen peas

**To serve:**

mashed potatoes (page 13)

**To garnish:**

chopped fresh curly parsley (optional)

Heat the vegetable oil in a large frying pan over a medium heat. Add the onion and cook for 8 minutes before adding the garlic and cooking for another 2 minutes.

Turn up the heat and add the beef mince. Break it up with a spoon but don't overmix or break it up too much – try to keep some texture. Allow it to get some colour before stirring it to brown all over. This will take 8–10 minutes.

Add the carrots and celery and cook for 2 minutes. Add the tomato purée and flour and cook for another 2 minutes, then stir in the stock, Worcestershire sauce, bay leaves and dried mixed herbs and season with salt and pepper. Bring to a boil, then reduce the heat and simmer for 20 minutes. Add the peas and cook for a final 5 minutes, adding a dash of water if it looks too dry.

Serve with lots of buttery mash on the side and garnish with chopped fresh curly parsley if you like.

# Variations

## FOOD FIGHT: SHEPHERD'S PIE VS. COTTAGE PIE

First things first: shepherd's pie is made with lamb or mutton, whereas cottage pie is made with beef.

### COTTAGE PIE

When you've finished cooking the savoury mince on page 108, preheat the oven to 180°C fan. Pour the mince into a large baking dish and allow to cool. Top with a layer of mashed potatoes that have been seasoned and mashed with butter and milk – see my Monday to Thursday mash on page 13. I also like to add a large spoonful of horseradish to the mash. Spoon the mash on top of the mince and use a fork to spread it out. Bake in the preheated oven for 20–25 minutes, until the mash is golden and the mince is bubbling.

## SHEPHERD'S PIE

Make the savoury mince as per the
recipe on page 108 but use lamb
or mutton mince instead of beef.
I like to add a large spoonful of
mint jelly or a few shredded fresh
mint leaves to the sauce at the end
before pouring the mince into a
large baking dish and allowing it to
cool. Using the Monday to Thursday
mash on page 13, spoon the mash
on top of the mince and use a fork
to spread it out. Bake in an oven
preheated to 180°C for 20–25
minutes, until the mash is golden
and the mince is bubbling.

# Hummus kawarma

This is one of those two-for-one recipes: you get a hummus recipe and you also get an option to bring that hummus to a whole new level. I've had hummus kawarma a few times from a Lebanese and Syrian restaurant in Dublin and loved it, but it wasn't until I went to Jerusalem with my dad and ate in a Lebanese restaurant close to the Holy Sepulchre that I really tasted how good this dish is: cool, creamy hummus topped with warm, crisp lamb, warming spices and finished with lots of fresh parsley, green chilli and lemon.

Serves 4

**For the hummus:**

1 x 400g tin of chickpeas, drained and rinsed

120g light tahini

3 garlic cloves, finely chopped

juice of 2 lemons

50–100ml ice-cold water

**For the lamb:**

25g butter

1 tsp vegetable oil

1 small onion, finely chopped

450g lamb mince

2 garlic cloves, finely chopped

1 tbsp dried mint

1 heaped tsp za'atar

1 tsp ground allspice

a good pinch of ground cinnamon

a good grating of nutmeg

a splash of water

juice of ½ lemon (cut the remaining half into wedges to serve)

To make the hummus, blitz the chickpeas, tahini, garlic and lemon juice together in a food processor. With the motor still running, slowly drizzle in ice-cold water just until you have a smooth, creamy consistency.

Spread the hummus across the base of a serving dish, creating a well in the middle that will become home to the warm spiced lamb. I put the serving dish and hummus in the fridge while I cook the lamb to allow it to cool a little, as I love the contrast between the cool hummus and the hot lamb.

For the lamb topping, heat the butter and oil in a large frying pan over a medium heat. When the butter has melted and is starting to foam, add the onion and cook for 6 minutes. Turn up the heat and add the lamb mince. Break it up with a spoon but don't overmix or break it up too much – try to keep some texture. Allow it to get some colour before stirring it to brown all over. This will take about 10 minutes.

Add the garlic and all the spices along with a splash of water. Stir everything together and cook for another 2–3 minutes, allowing the water to evaporate. Turn off the heat and finish by mixing in the lemon juice, chilli and parsley.

To serve, spoon all the lamb and any juices from the pan into the well in the hummus. Serve with warm pitta or flatbreads on the side and the lemon wedges for a final squeeze.

1 fresh green chilli,
deseeded and finely
chopped

a small handful of fresh
parsley, finely chopped

**To serve:**

warm pitta or flatbreads
(page 11)

# Irish stew

I'm sitting at the dining table in my parents' kitchen. Mum is unpacking the shopping after a quick trip to the supermarket and I'd gone to FX Buckley's on Moore Street in Dublin before getting the train to Athy. I have brought the gigot lamb chops and the streaky bacon and Mum is unpacking the carrots, potatoes and celery. She gets out a few onions and opens the press to get the salt, white pepper and curry powder. Believe it or not, we're making Irish stew – with curry powder!

I've watched Mum make stew plenty of times in the past and know that she always adds curry powder. For years I never questioned it – I thought everyone put curry powder in their stew. But after having a chat about it with Mum, I discovered that she learned to make stew from my Granny Flynn, who loved cooking and was a great one for adding different flavours and spices to her food, one being curry powder in her Irish stew.

Now to be clear, the stew doesn't taste like curry. The powder just adds a subtle base note to the stew, a layer of flavour that you can't quite put your finger on. Think of it as the secret ingredient.

Serves 6

6 gigot lamb chops on the bone

500g streaky bacon

10 medium-sized floury potatoes (see page 14), peeled

2 medium onions, roughly chopped

4 carrots, roughly chopped

4 celery sticks, roughly chopped

1 generous tsp curry powder

salt and ground white pepper

Preheat the oven to 190°C fan.

Prepare the lamb by trimming off any excess fat and cutting the meat into bite-sized pieces. Keep the bones, as these will be added to the stew for extra flavour.

To prepare the streaky bacon, remove and discard the rind (skin) and cut the bacon into bite-sized pieces.

Cut four of the potatoes into small cubes. Keep the remaining six potatoes whole for later in the recipe.

Put the lamb, bacon, the four cubed potatoes and the onions, carrots and celery in a heavy-based casserole that has a lid. Season with the curry powder and a pinch of salt and ground white pepper. Pour in the stock and give everything a good mix. Put the pot on a high heat and bring to a boil, then cover with the lid and transfer to the oven. Reduce the temperature to 180°C fan and cook for 1¾ hours.

While the stew is cooking, parboil the whole potatoes in salted water for 20 minutes. →

750ml–1 litre lamb stock, depending on how thick you like your stew

1 small bunch of fresh curly parsley, finely chopped

Remove the casserole from the oven and give the stew a good stir to break down the potatoes and thicken the sauce. Nestle the parboiled whole potatoes into the stew, put the lid back on and return to the oven to cook for another 15–20 minutes, until the whole potatoes are completely cooked through and the meat is tender. Remove from the oven and allow to stand for 15 minutes.

Serve in warm bowls with a sprinkling of fresh parsley and an obligatory glass of cold milk.

# Lamb tagine
## with couscous

I have eaten many a tagine over the years, especially during my time spent in Morocco. I adore Morocco, especially its food. I don't think there is anywhere as provocative in terms of food as an evening in Jemaa el-Fnaa Square in Marrakech. During the day the square is filled with orange juice carts and water sellers with their brass cups and leather water bags, as well as mobile barbers and snake charmers. As the late afternoon approaches, magicians, storytellers and dancers start to arrive. But for me, the real magic happens as darkness falls, when the crowds increase and dozens of restaurants mysteriously appear out of nowhere with their strings of lights, open fires and pots bubbling away, offering harira soup, merguez sausage, fish with chermoula, mint tea, lots of different sheep bits, and of course tagine and couscous. Morocco, and especially Jemaa el-Fnaa Square, is a feast for all the senses.

Serves 4

600g lamb, from the shoulder, leg or shanks, trimmed and diced

4 tbsp vegetable oil

2 tbsp ras el hanout (page 14)

2 tsp ground cinnamon

1 tsp ground ginger

2 medium onions, thinly sliced

2 garlic cloves, finely chopped

1 x 400g tin of chopped tomatoes

1 orange, 4 strips of rind removed with a vegetable peeler and the juice

Put the lamb in a large bowl with 2 tablespoons of the oil and the ras el hanout, cinnamon and ginger. Use clean hands to massage everything together. Cover with cling film and refrigerate for at least 2 hours.

Preheat the oven to 160°C fan.

In a tagine or a heavy-based casserole, heat the remaining 2 tablespoons of oil over a medium heat. Add the onions and cook for 10 minutes before adding the garlic and cooking for a further 5 minutes. Turn up the heat slightly and add the marinated lamb, then continue to cook for 5 minutes more, stirring occasionally, until the meat browns all over.

Deglaze the pan with a dash of cold water. Pour in the tin of chopped tomatoes and add the orange rind and juice, rosemary and chilli and season with salt and pepper, stirring to combine. Put the lid on the tagine or casserole and cook in the preheated oven for 1½ hours.

Towards the end of the cooking time, make the couscous according to the packet instructions. When it's done, fluff it up with a fork and flavour it with lots of shredded fresh mint and the lemon zest and juice. ⊙

1 sprig of fresh
rosemary

1 fresh red chilli,
pierced with a sharp
knife several times

salt and freshly
ground black pepper

75g slivered almonds

100g dried apricots,
cut in half

100g Medjool dates,
stoned and cut in half

2 tbsp honey

**To serve:**

freshly cooked
couscous

shredded fresh mint
leaves

zest and juice of
1 lemon

Put the almonds in a small baking dish.

Remove the lamb from the oven and gently stir in
the apricots, dates and honey. Taste and add more
salt and pepper if required. Return to the oven along
with the dish of almonds for another 15 minutes.

To serve, spoon a bed of couscous into each serving
bowl. Divide the tagine among the bowls and top with
the toasted almonds.

# Beef & Guinness stew

In much the same way that many traditional Irish desserts are served with a dollop of softly whipped cream (something you'll never hear me complain about!), many traditional Irish savoury dishes seem to be served with a big scoop of mash (again, something you will never hear me complain about!). If you want to take this classic to another level, serve it with Guinness mustard mash, made using your own homemade Guinness mustard.

The Guinness in this beef stew not only adds a deep, rich flavour but gives it a deep colour too. To intensify that flavour even more, I add smoked bacon.

Serves 4–6

3 tbsp vegetable oil

1kg diced stewing beef

125g smoked bacon lardons

1 onion, roughly chopped

3 carrots, cut into chunks

3 celery sticks, cut into chunks

2 garlic cloves, finely chopped

2 tbsp plain flour

2 tbsp tomato purée

500ml Guinness stout

100ml beef stock made with 1 stock cube

1 tbsp homemade Guinness mustard (see the next page) or shop-bought wholegrain mustard

3 bay leaves

1 sprig of fresh thyme (reserve a few leaves for garnish)

To make the mustard, put the yellow and black mustard seeds in a non-metallic bowl and pour over the Guinness. Cover with cling film and leave at room temperature for three days.

Pour the mustard seeds into a fine mesh sieve set over a bowl. Blend half of the seeds in a food processor to break them down, then transfer them to a clean bowl along with the remaining whole seeds and the vinegar, salt and honey. Thoroughly mix together, adding a little of the reserved liquid if it's too thick. Store in a sterilised jar (see page 17) at room temperature and use within one month.

To make the beef and Guinness stew, preheat the oven to 140°C fan.

Heat 1½ tablespoons of the oil in a large heavy-based casserole over a medium-high heat. Working in batches, add the meat and brown it all over. Transfer to a plate with a slotted spoon and set aside.

Add the remaining 1½ tablespoons of oil, then add the bacon lardons and fry until golden. Add the onion, carrots and celery and cook for about 5 minutes. Add the flour and tomato purée and cook for 1 minute more. Add the beef back in, including any juices from the plate, along with the Guinness, stock and mustard and give everything a good mix. Using a spoon, push the bay leaves and thyme into the stew.

Cover the casserole with a lid and transfer to the preheated oven. Cook for 2–3 hours, until the meat is very tender.

Serve in warm shallow bowls with a side of mash that has been flavoured with some of the Guinness mustard and garnish with a few fresh thyme leaves.

**For the Guinness mustard:**

50g yellow mustard seeds

50g black mustard seeds

250ml Guinness

40ml malt vinegar

1 tsp salt

2 tsp honey

**To serve:**

mashed potatoes (page 13)

# Beef & lemongrass stew
## with coconut rice

One of the joys of the modern world we live in is that you no longer have to travel to try amazing food. Have the food of Alex and Richie of Bahay and you'll be transported to the Philippines. Sham Hanifa will bring you to Malaysia, while Kwanghi Chan, who was born in Hong Kong, will give you a flavour of China. Or take a walk down Capel Street in Dublin and you can eat food from Vietnam (Aobaba), Korea (Arisu) or Japan (Musashi). I have travelled a little in Asia and am lucky to have been to Vietnam, Cambodia and Thailand. A dish that always stands out in my mind is a beef and lemongrass stew with coconut rice that I had in Bangkok. Inspired by the fragrant flavours of that dish, this is my version.

Serves 4

6 lemongrass stalks

5 garlic cloves, peeled

2.5cm piece of ginger, peeled and chopped

2 fresh red chillies, deseeded and thinly sliced

1 bunch of fresh coriander, leaves and stalks separated

2 tbsp vegetable oil

1kg diced stewing beef

1 medium onion, thinly sliced

1 x 400ml tin of coconut milk

400ml beef stock

4 tbsp soy sauce

2 tbsp light brown sugar

Preheat the oven to 160°C fan.

Remove the outer leaves from the lemongrass stalks and discard them, then coarsely chop the stalks. Make a paste by blitzing the lemongrass, garlic, ginger, three-quarters of the chillies and all the coriander stalks in a food processor.

Heat the oil in a large heavy-based casserole over a medium-high heat. Working in batches, add the beef and brown it all over. Use a slotted spoon to transfer the browned beef to a plate and set aside.

Add the onion and cook for about 5 minutes, until starting to soften, then add all of the paste and cook for another 3–4 minutes to release the flavours. Stir in the browned beef along with the coconut milk, stock, soy sauce and sugar and bring to a boil. Cover with a lid and transfer to the preheated oven to cook for 1½–2 hours, until the meat is very tender.

To make the coconut rice, heat the oil in a medium-sized casserole that has a lid over a medium heat. Add the onion and cook for 5 minutes, then add the rice and cook for 2 minutes. Stir in the coconut milk, then fill the tin with the water, swish it around and stir that into the rice too. Cover the dish with a lid and transfer to the oven to cook alongside the stew for the final 30 minutes of the stew's cooking time. When the rice is done, fluff it up using a fork and gently mix in the lime zest. ⊙

**For the coconut rice:**

1 tbsp vegetable oil

1 medium onion, finely chopped

300g jasmine rice

1 x 400ml tin of coconut milk

400ml water

zest of 1 lime

**To serve:**

1 lime, cut into wedges

Serve the beef in warm bowls on a bed of coconut rice with the lime wedges on the side for squeezing over. Garnish with a scattering of fresh coriander leaves and the remaining slivers of chilli.

# Steak & kidney pie

One of the biggest conflicts in my life is the debate about who makes the best steak and kidney pie: my mother or my mother-in-law. In one you have the most beautiful sauce packed with steak, mushrooms and the delicate flavour of lamb kidneys all topped with a flaky puff pastry, while in the other you have a more robust filling with beef kidneys and a topping of suet pastry. It's actually not really a conflict at all, as I love both of their pies. So I've taken the best of both and married them together – just like their sons.

Steak and kidney pie is a labour of love that you need to start the day before you want to serve it, but it's worth it.

Serves 6

**For the filling:**

300g lamb kidneys
(4–5 kidneys)

4 tbsp vegetable oil

1 large onion, roughly chopped

75g plain flour

salt and freshly ground black pepper

1kg diced stewing steak or stewing beef

50g butter, plus extra for greasing

250g button mushrooms, cleaned and cut in half (see page 13)

600ml hot beef stock

1 bay leaf

**For the pastry:**

400g self-raising flour, plus extra for dusting

200g beef suet, shredded

250–275ml cold water

1 egg, beaten

Preheat the oven to 140°C fan.

To make the filling, cut the kidneys into bite-sized pieces, trimming away any of the white central core.

Heat 1 tablespoon of the oil in a large frying pan over a medium-high heat. Add the kidneys and cook until they are golden all over, then use a slotted spoon to transfer them to a large, heavy-based casserole.

Reduce the heat to medium and add 1 more tablespoon of oil. Add the onion and cook for 8 minutes, until slightly golden, then transfer to the casserole with the slotted spoon. Give the frying pan a quick clean.

Put the flour in a large, clean ziplock bag and season well with salt and pepper. Add the beef to the bag and shake well to coat it with the seasoned flour.

Heat 1 tablespoon of oil and half of the butter in the frying pan over a medium-high heat. When the butter has melted and is starting to foam, add the beef to the pan in batches to brown it all over, being careful not to overcrowd the pan. Transfer each batch to the casserole when it's done.

Add the remaining tablespoon of oil and the remaining butter to the frying pan. Add the mushrooms and cook for about 4 minutes, until they have taken on a little colour. Add these to the casserole along with any remaining flour from the ziplock bag, the hot beef stock and the bay leaf and give everything ➔

a good stir. Cover the casserole with a lid and transfer to the preheated oven to cook for 2–2½ hours, until the meat is very tender. Allow to cool before popping in the fridge overnight.

The next day, preheat the oven to 180°C fan. Grease a 30cm x 22cm pie dish generously with butter.

To make the pastry, simply mix the flour, suet and a good pinch of salt with 250ml of cold water in a large bowl. Use the blade of a butter knife to bring everything together, adding the remaining 25ml of cold water if needed.

Tip the dough out onto a clean lightly floured surface and knead gently for 1 minute. Reserve two-thirds of the pastry for the lid. Roll out the remaining third thinly and cut it into long strips about 5cm wide and 8cm long. Put the strips in the pie dish so that they are going up the sides and overhanging the rim slightly. You don't line the bottom of this pie with pastry, as it would get too soggy.

Spoon the filling into the lined pie dish. Roll out the remaining pastry to make a lid for the pie. Brush the rim of the dough with a little water before draping over the lid and pinching the edges together to seal. If you're not baking the pie immediately, cover it lightly with cling film and keep it in the fridge until you're ready to bake. The pie can be made up to 24 hours in advance up to this stage.

Using the tip of a sharp knife, make four small cuts across the top of the pie before brushing with the beaten egg. Bake in the preheated oven for 20 minutes, then turn down the temperature to 160°C fan and bake for a further 20–25 minutes, until the pie is golden brown and the filling is bubbling. Remove from the oven and allow to stand for 10 minutes before serving.

I rarely give drink pairing recommendations, as I leave that to my husband, Daithí – his knowledge and appreciation of wines is outstanding. But steak and kidney pie should always be served with a big glass of cold milk!

## Note

Be sure to make the filling the day before. You need the filling to be cold so that the pastry doesn't melt when it's added to it.

# Meat & two veg
## (plus a potato because we're Irish)

What would your last supper be? Your death row meal? I like to think that I would go for something decadent and luxurious like lobster, caviar, black truffle and champagne, but honestly, meat and two veg (or even the veg and two veg on page 138!) is my perfect meal. It's a plate of some of my all-time favourite foods that are warming, comforting and full of flavour: roast chicken, cauliflower cheese, carrot and parsnip mash, roast baby potatoes and gravy. I love nothing more than cooking these dishes for my family and friends, sitting around a big dining table sharing stories, laughs and time together. So whatever your last supper or death row meal is, eat more of what makes you happy – and share it with friends and family, making memories.

Serves 4–6

**For the roast chicken:**

1 onion, peeled and cut into wedges

2 carrots, peeled and cut lengthways

1 x 1.5–2kg free-range chicken (1.5kg to serve 4 or 2kg to serve 6)

salt and freshly ground black pepper

1 lemon, halved

1 small bunch of fresh thyme

vegetable oil

**Roast chicken:** Preheat the oven to 180°C fan. Put the onion and carrots in the bottom of a roasting tray that comfortably fits the chicken but is not too big. Season the inside of the chicken cavity with salt and pepper and stuff with the lemon and thyme. Drizzle the outside of the chicken with a little vegetable oil and season with salt and pepper, rubbing the seasoning and oil into the skin with your hands. Put the chicken directly on top of the vegetables, then transfer the tray to the preheated oven and roast for 1½ hours for a 1.5kg chicken or 1¾ hours for a 2kg chicken.

To check that the chicken is cooked, use a knife to pierce the thigh meat: the juices should run clear, with no trace of pink. If there is, return it to the oven to cook for 5–10 minutes more. Allow the juices from the chicken cavity to drain into the roasting tray (keep these veg and juices for the gravy), then transfer the chicken to a chopping board to rest for 15–20 minutes.

**Gravy:** Melt the butter in a saucepan over a medium heat. When it starts to foam, add the flour and cook for 2–3 minutes to make a roux. Slowly add the stock along with the contents of the roasting tray, including the vegetables. Simmer for a few minutes before straining through a fine mesh sieve into another saucepan. Keep warm. Be sure to add any extra juices that have collected on the chopping board from the resting chicken before serving. ⊕

**For the gravy:**

25g butter

1 tbsp plain flour

250ml chicken stock

**For the roast baby potatoes:**

1.5kg baby potatoes

3 tbsp vegetable oil

1 full garlic bulb, cut in half through the middle

a few sprigs of fresh rosemary

**For the cauliflower cheese:**

1 large cauliflower, cut into florets

1 batch of cheese sauce (page 10)

50g grated red Cheddar

**For the carrot & parsnip mash:**

3 large carrots, peeled

2 large parsnips, peeled

50g butter

50ml cream

1 sprig of fresh rosemary

ground white pepper

**Roast baby potatoes:** Put the potatoes, oil, garlic and rosemary in a roasting tray, season with salt and pepper and toss everything together. Roast in the oven for 45–60 minutes, until golden and slightly wrinkly.

**Cauliflower cheese:** Bring a large pan of salted water to a boil. Add the cauliflower florets and cook for 6–8 minutes, until tender. Drain the cauliflower and arrange it in a baking dish. Pour the cheese sauce over the cauliflower and scatter over the grated cheese. Bake in the oven for 20 minutes, until the cheese is golden and the sauce is bubbling.

**Carrot & parsnip mash:** Dice the carrots and parsnips into even-sized pieces and add to a pan of cold water with a good pinch of salt. Bring to a boil, then reduce the heat slightly. Cook for about 15 minutes, until they are tender. Drain into a colander and allow to steam dry for a few minutes. Put the butter, cream and rosemary in the same pan that you cooked the veg in and warm gently over a medium heat. Remove the rosemary and add the cooked carrots and parsnips, then mash together and season with salt and white pepper. Transfer to a serving dish and keep warm until ready to serve.

To serve, carve the chicken by removing the legs and slicing off the breast fillets, then arrange them on a warm serving platter or plates. I like to serve everything else family style in separate bowls in the middle of the table, with everyone helping themselves.

# Timings

You need to give yourself 2½ hours to prepare this meal. If you want to eat at 7 p.m., these would be your timings.

**4:30:** Take the chicken out of the fridge and prepare. Make the cheese sauce for the cauliflower. Preheat the oven.

**5:00:** Put the chicken in the oven. Cook the cauliflower and arrange it in the baking dish with the sauce and grated cheese. Prepare your potatoes and have them ready for the oven. Peel and chop your carrots and parsnips.

**6:00:** Put the potatoes in the oven.

**6:25:** Start cooking the carrots and parsnips.

**6:30:** Check/remove the chicken from the oven. Finish the carrot and parsnip mash and keep warm on a low heat, stirring occasionally.

**6:40:** Put the cauliflower in the oven and make the gravy.

**7:00:** Remove everything from the oven and transfer to warm serving bowls and platters.

# Veg
# ~~Meat~~ & two veg
## (plus a potato because we're Irish)

Meat shouldn't always be the main attraction. With a little imagination, you can make the vegetables the star. Vegetables deserve to be celebrated in exactly the same way as a piece of meat does, so I've taken the same veg from the traditional meat and two veg on pages 134–137 and put them centre stage. I've also used some of my favourite ingredients that are now widely available in Ireland, like ras el hanout, pomegranate seeds and miso, to transform these everyday vegetables into something special.

Serves 4–6

**For the whole roasted ras el hanout cauliflower:**

1 large cauliflower, outer leaves removed

3 tbsp vegetable oil

3 garlic cloves, finely chopped

1 tbsp ras el hanout (page 14)

100g Greek yogurt

50g almond butter

juice of ½ lemon

a small handful of fresh parsley, finely chopped, to serve

seeds from 1 pomegranate, to serve

toasted flaked almonds, to serve

**Whole roasted ras el hanout cauliflower:** Preheat the oven to 180°C fan. Using a large saucepan that's big enough to fit the whole cauliflower and that has a lid, fill it with water until it reaches a depth of about 5cm. Add a good pinch of salt and bring to a boil, then carefully lower the whole cauliflower into the pan so that it's sitting in the water base side down. Cover the pan with the lid and boil for 5 minutes. This allows the cauliflower to partially cook before roasting. Carefully remove the cauliflower from the water and allow it to steam dry.

Mix the vegetable oil with the garlic and ras el hanout in a small bowl. Put the cauliflower in a roasting tray and brush it liberally with the flavoured oil, making sure the bottom of the cauliflower is coated too. Reserve a little oil for a second coat later.

Transfer the tray to the preheated oven and roast for 15 minutes. Remove from the oven and brush the cauliflower with the reserved oil, then roast for a further 25–30 minutes, until it's golden and slightly crisp.

To make the dressing, whisk the yogurt, almond butter and lemon juice together in a small bowl.

Spread some of the yogurt dressing on a serving dish. Put the roasted cauliflower on top of the yogurt on the dish, then drizzle over the rest of the yogurt and add a scattering of parsley, pomegranate seeds and toasted flaked almonds. ⊕

**For the roast carrots with yogurt & fennel:**

300g carrots, halved lengthways

1 fennel bulb, cut into 8 wedges (keep the green fronds to serve)

1 tbsp good-quality olive oil, plus extra to serve

1 tsp coriander seeds, crushed

1 tsp fennel seeds, crushed

½ tsp chilli flakes

300g Greek yogurt

2 garlic cloves, finely chopped

**For the hasselback miso parsnips:**

6 parsnips, cut in half lengthways

2 tbsp olive oil

salt and freshly ground black pepper

2 large tbsp miso

1 tbsp honey

**For the buttermilk mash:**

1kg floury potatoes (see page 14), peeled and cut into chunks

50g butter, plus extra for serving

100ml buttermilk

salt and ground white pepper

1 small bunch of fresh chives, finely chopped

**Roast carrot, fennel & yogurt:** Preheat the oven to 180°C fan. In a large bowl, toss the carrots and fennel wedges with the olive oil, coriander seeds, fennel seeds, chilli flakes and a generous pinch of salt, making sure everything is well coated. Transfer to a baking tray and roast in the oven for 25–30 minutes, until tender.

In a small bowl, mix the yogurt with the garlic and some of the fennel fronds, then spread this onto a serving dish. When the carrots and fennel are cooked, arrange them on top of the yogurt. Scatter with the remaining fennel fronds and drizzle with a little olive oil.

**Hasselback miso parsnips:** Preheat the oven to 180°C fan. Line a baking tray with non-stick baking paper. Using a sharp knife, carefully make deep cuts in each parsnip at 5mm intervals all along the length, taking care not to cut all the way through. Brush the bottom of each parsnip with a little olive oil and arrange on the lined tray. Brush the top of each one with more oil and season. Roast in the preheated oven for 15 minutes.

Mix the miso with the remining oil and the honey to form a paste, adding a dash of water if it's too thick. Brush this over the parsnips and roast for a further 25 minutes, brushing them one or two more times with the glaze during this cooking time. They are ready to serve when they are golden and tender.

**Buttermilk mash:** Put the potatoes in the top of a steamer and season with salt. Steam over a pan of boiling water for 20–25 minutes, until tender. Remove the steamer from the pot and allow the potatoes to steam dry for a few minutes, then pour away the water.

Add the butter and buttermilk to the same pan and warm gently over a medium heat. Remove the pan from the heat, add the potatoes and mash together. Season with salt and white pepper and mix through the chives. Serve in a warm bowl with more butter on top.

# Timings

You need to give yourself 2 hours to prepare this meal. If you wanted to eat at 7 p.m., these would be your timings.

**5:00:** Prepare the different elements of the dishes by pre-cooking the cauliflower and mixing the oil, garlic and spices together. Prepare the carrots and fennel and make the dressing. Peel and cut the parsnips and make the glaze. Peel the potatoes and keep them covered with cold water until you're ready to cook.

**6:00:** Preheat the oven. Finish preparing the cauliflower and parsnips for the oven.

**6:15:** Put the cauliflower in the oven. Put the potatoes on to cook. Finish preparing the carrots and fennel for the oven.

**6:30:** Put the carrots and fennel in the oven. Glaze the cauliflower and the parsnips.

**6:45:** Finish the buttermilk mash and keep warm on a low heat.

**7:00:** Remove everything from the oven and transfer to warm serving bowls and platters.

# Colcannon

When I was a little boy, one of my favourite toys was my Cabbage Patch Kid. I can't remember what his name was, but I can still clearly see him, with his light brown woollen hair and his bright blue eyes. Both our birthdays were registered, and every year a birthday card would come in the post. I even had different clothes for him. I think he really was my first best friend as a young boy.

The reason I mention this is because it is a well-known fact that babies in Ireland are found in the cabbage patch. Ireland has so many cabbage traditions. For example, young women would be blindfolded and would then head out to pick a cabbage on 31 October. The cabbage roots would describe the type of person she would marry: long, short, fat, thin, hairy, dirty, etc. The cabbage would then be cooked and mixed with potatoes to make colcannon, which would have a ring mixed into it. The person who found it would be the next one to get married. When we were growing up, Mum would add coins wrapped in parchment paper to the colcannon for us to find instead.

Serves 6

1kg potatoes, peeled and cut into even-sized pieces

150g butter, plus extra for serving

2 tablespoons water

250g curly kale or savoy cabbage, tough stalks removed and discarded and the leaves thinly sliced

100ml cream

salt and freshly ground black pepper

Cook the potatoes by either steaming them or putting them in a saucepan of cold salted water and bringing to a boil, then reducing to a simmer until cooked through and tender.

While the potatoes are cooking, put a large frying pan on a medium heat. Add about 25g of the butter and the water. When the butter has melted, add the kale or cabbage and give it a good toss to coat. Cook, shaking the pan regularly, for about 5 minutes, until the kale or cabbage is softened but is still bright green.

When the potatoes are cooked, remove them from the steamer or drain and allow to steam dry for 5 minutes.

Add the remaining butter and the cream to the saucepan and warm gently over a medium heat. Add the potatoes and mash together. Season with salt and pepper and stir in the kale or cabbage.

Serve in a large bowl with extra butter added on top.

# Celeriac, brown butter & pear mash

I love a mash with a twist, like the mash with homemade Guinness mustard on page 122 or this celeriac and pear mash, which works well with the roast pork belly on page 102. Other vegetables that work for this type of mash include carrots, parsnips, swedes, turnips – most root vegetables, really – as well as pumpkin and squash. The addition of the brown butter adds a beautiful nutty flavour to the mash.

Another great mash with a twist is roast garlic mash, especially if you already have the oven on. Simply rub a whole head of garlic with 1 tablespoon of olive oil and wrap the whole head in a piece of foil. Pop it in the oven for 30 minutes, open up the parcel and allow to cool slightly before cutting the garlic in half and squeezing out all the glorious sweet roasted goodness. Mash all the roasted garlic into your potatoes with the butter and cream.

Serves 6

500g floury potatoes (see page 14), peeled and cut into even-sized pieces

500g celeriac, peeled and cut into even-sized pieces

4 pears, peeled, cored and cut into quarters

3 tbsp water

125g butter, plus extra for serving

3 tbsp crème fraîche

salt and ground white pepper

**To garnish:**

finely chopped fresh chives

Cook the potatoes by either steaming them or putting them in a saucepan of cold salted water and bringing to a boil, then reducing to a simmer until cooked through and tender. Either way, add the celeriac for the last 15 minutes of cooking

While the potatoes are cooking, put a small saucepan that has a lid over a medium heat. Add the pears and water, cover the pan with the lid and cook for about 10 minutes. The pears should break down and look a little fluffy when cooked.

When the potatoes and celeriac are cooked, remove them from the steamer or drain and allow to steam dry for 10 minutes.

Meanwhile, add the butter to the saucepan and put the pan back on a medium heat. Allow the butter to melt and foam up, stirring occasionally. The milk solids in the butter are going to toast and turn golden brown, which will give the butter a deep nutty flavour. This will take between 6 and 10 minutes, but be careful not to let the butter burn. You'll know it's done when the butter goes quiet in the pan and it smells nutty. Set aside a little brown butter to pour over the finished mash at the end.

Add the potatoes and celeriac back to the saucepan with the brown butter, crème fraîche and cooked pears. Season with salt and white pepper and mash together.

Serve in a large bowl with the reserved brown butter poured over and garnish with finely chopped fresh chives.

# Tea

# Egg in a window

I talk about childhood favourites a lot in this book and this was definitely one of them – and still is to this day. If I need to eat something in a hurry or simply want a little bit of comfort, this is my go-to dish. As I was researching this recipe, I was amazed to discover so many different names for this dish – egg in a hole, bull's eye egg, gashouse egg, one-eyed Jack, pirate's eye – but I couldn't find a single reference to egg in a window. Maybe that's just what it was called in our house.

Serves 1

1 slice of slightly stale bread

20g butter

a dash of oil

1 egg

salt and freshly ground black pepper

**To serve:**

ketchup, sriracha, peanut rayu or whatever you like with your eggs

Using the rim of a glass or a circular cutter, cut a hole from the centre of the bread.

Put the butter and oil in a frying pan over a medium heat. When the butter has melted, put the bread in the pan – both the 'window' and the circle that you cut out. Crack the egg into the centre of the hole in the slice of bread. Season the egg with a little salt and pepper.

Cook until the egg is set a little and the bread is golden brown. This will take a couple of minutes. Flip both over and cook for another minute or so, until the bread is golden and the egg white is set.

Serve both the 'window' and the circle with a dollop of tomato ketchup on the side for dipping, a drizzle of sriracha, a spoonful of peanut rayu or whatever you like to have with your eggs.

## Note

Do try to use slightly stale bread, as it tends to fry more evenly.

# Anda bhurji

I first had this Indian dish many years ago in Delhi O'Deli on Moore Street in Dublin. Unfortunately the restaurant is no longer there but I still remember the food, with a depth of flavour and a lightness that were mind-blowing. On our first visit, my husband Daithí and I were shocked when we left and realised we had just inadvertently had an entirely vegetarian meal. Note to self: must add trip to India to my bucket list!

Serves 2

3 eggs

1 tbsp milk

1½ tbsp vegetable oil

1 tsp cumin seeds

1 large onion, finely chopped

2 garlic cloves, finely chopped

1–2 fresh green chillies (depending on how hot you like your food), finely chopped

2 ripe tomatoes, deseeded and diced

1 tsp paprika

½ tsp ground turmeric

salt and ground white pepper

**To serve:**

1 small bunch of fresh coriander, leaves only

warm naan or flatbreads (page 11)

Beat the eggs with the milk in a small bowl.

Heat the oil in a large frying pan over a medium heat. Add the cumin seeds and fry for 15 seconds to release their flavour. Add the onion and cook for 5 minutes, then add the garlic and chilli and cook for another 3 minutes. Add the tomatoes, paprika and turmeric and cook for 5 minutes more.

Add the beaten eggs along with some salt and ground white pepper and give everything a good shake. Let the mixture sit in the pan undisturbed for about 15 seconds, then using a spatula, gently move the eggs around the pan. Let the mixture sit for another 15 seconds, then stir with the spatula again. Repeat this process until the eggs are softly set and still a little wet, as the eggs will continue to cook for another minute or so off the heat.

Serve with a generous scattering of fresh coriander leaves and some warm naan or flatbreads.

# Fish fingers, peas & chips

We were a pork and bacon butcher, but every Friday we sold fish in our shop. Mum would use a white marker to list that week's offering on the shop window. My favourite was always whiting, which Mum would simply dust with seasoned flour and fry in butter. My other favourite was homemade fish fingers, always served with peas and chips. I'm also partial to the ones from the freezer aisle as well – they make great sandwiches!

Serves 4

**For the fish fingers:**

100g plain flour

3 eggs, beaten

200g fresh white breadcrumbs

salt and freshly ground black pepper

1 x 600g piece of skinned chunky white fish such as cod, haddock, pollock or ling, cut into 12 fingers

vegetable oil, for deep-frying

**For the crushed peas:**

200g frozen peas

25g butter

**To serve:**

chips (page 180 or shop-bought)

lemon wedges

tartar sauce (see the note)

Preheat the oven to 120°C fan.

Start by getting everything ready to coat your fish fingers. Put the flour, beaten eggs and breadcrumbs in three separate wide, shallow dishes. Season the flour with salt and pepper.

Preheat the oil in your deep-fryer to 180°C.

Working with one piece of fish at a time, first dip it in the flour, followed by the egg and finally the breadcrumbs, making sure the fish is completely covered each time. Put the crumbed fish finger on a plate while you work on the rest. And here's a little tip: keep one hand wet and the other hand dry, so in other words, use one hand to pick up the fish and take it out of the egg, then use the other hand to remove it from the flour and breadcrumbs.

When you're ready to cook, carefully put three or four fish fingers in the fryer basket and lower it into the hot oil. Cook for about 5 minutes, until the fish is cooked and the crumb coating is crisp and golden brown. Transfer to an ovenproof plate lined with kitchen paper and keep warm in the preheated oven while you cook the rest of the fish fingers.

Cook the peas in boiling water for 5 minutes, then drain and return to the saucepan with the butter and some salt and pepper. Use a potato masher to roughly mash the peas.

Serve the fish fingers with the crushed peas, chips, a lemon wedge and tartar sauce.

*Note* Make a simple tartar sauce by mixing
4 tablespoons of mayonnaise with
1 large, finely chopped gherkin, the juice
of half a lemon, a little chopped scallion
and some chopped fresh parsley.

# Fish fingers, peas & chips 2.0

I'm taking a bit of creative licence with this version, which is all about the contrast of textures. Yes, we're making fish fingers, but they're salmon. Yes, we're making peas, but it's a rich, creamy, smoky pea fricassée. Yes, we're making chips, but in the American way: we're having crisps for our tea!

Serves 2

**For the fish fingers:**

50g plain flour

2 eggs, beaten

100g fresh white breadcrumbs

salt and freshly ground black pepper

1 x 300g piece of fresh skinless salmon, cut into 6 fingers

vegetable oil, for deep-frying

**For the pea fricassée:**

1 tbsp vegetable oil

50g butter

1 medium onion, finely chopped

125g smoked bacon lardons

2 garlic cloves, finely chopped

200g frozen peas

100ml water

1 small bunch of fresh parsley, finely chopped

2 tbsp crème fraîche

Preheat the oven to 120°C fan.

Start by getting everything ready to coat your salmon fingers. Put the flour, beaten eggs and breadcrumbs in three separate wide, shallow dishes. Season the flour with salt and pepper.

Cut the potatoes into thin slices (a mandolin is best for this but the slicing attachment on a food processor will also work) and soak in cold water while you work on the other parts of the dish.

Working with one piece of salmon at a time, first dip it in the flour, followed by the egg and finally the breadcrumbs, making sure the fish is completely covered each time. Put the crumbed fish finger on a plate while you work on the rest. And here's a little tip: keep one hand wet and the other hand dry, so in other words, use one hand to pick up the fish and take it out of the egg, then use the other hand to remove it from the flour and breadcrumbs.

Preheat the oil in your deep-fryer to 180°C.

While the oil is heating up, make your fricassée. Heat the oil and half of the butter in a medium-sized frying pan. When the butter has melted and is starting to foam, add the onion and bacon and turn the heat up a little. Cook, stirring occasionally, for about 8 minutes, until the bacon is slightly crisp and the onion is golden. Add the garlic and cook for 2 minutes, then stir in the peas and water. Reduce the heat to a simmer – you want all the water to evaporate from the peas, which will allow them to cook but retain all their flavour. ⊙

## For the crisps:

2 medium potatoes, peeled

1 tsp salt and vinegar seasoning (page 16)

## To serve:

lemon wedges

While the peas are cooking, remove the potato slices from the water and dry them very well on a clean tea towel. Working with just a handful of slices at a time – don't be tempted to do too many at once! – cook in the deep-fryer until they are crisp and golden. Drain on kitchen paper while you cook the next batch. When they are all cooked, sprinkle them with the salt and vinegar seasoning.

To finish the fricassée, once all the water has evaporated, reduce the heat to low, add the remaining butter and stir in the parsley and crème fraîche, allowing the butter to melt and the crème fraîche to warm through. Keep warm.

When you're ready to cook the salmon fingers, carefully put three or four fish fingers into the fryer basket and lower it into the hot oil. Cook for about 5 minutes, until the fish is cooked and the crumb coating is crisp and golden brown. Transfer to an ovenproof plate lined with kitchen paper and keep warm in the preheated oven while you cook the rest of the fish fingers.

To serve, divide the fricassée between two plates and top each portion with three salmon fingers. I like to serve some of the crisps on top of the salmon and the rest on the side, using them to scoop up the peas. Add a lemon wedge for squeezing over the fish fingers.

# Mammy salad

Irish salad, salad plate or mammy salad – no matter what you call it, summer in Ireland wouldn't be complete without it. What goes on your salad plate is completely up to you, but in our house a salad plate would always be served with a big bowl of new season Irish potatoes. I've broken it down into different sections but choose what you want. There is no right or wrong when it comes to a salad plate, though there are a couple of rules: meats must be rolled up and cheese must be cut into triangles.

## THE MEATS

Slices of cooked ham, turkey or any other cooked meat. The only rule is that they have to be rolled up. I also love some roast chicken as part of a salad plate, especially if you can get it at that sweet spot moment when it's been out of the oven for about an hour and it's not quite cold but not quite hot either and the meat is like jelly.

## THE SIMPLE SALADS

**Lettuce:** Traditionally a few leaves of butterhead. I think this and iceberg were the only lettuce in Ireland until the 1990s.

**Tomatoes:** Ripe, room-temperature tomatoes cut into wedges with a little salt to season.

**Cucumber:** Cold from the fridge and simply cut into slices – or if it was a fancy plate, peeled, deseeded and cut into half-moon slices.

**Scallions:** Simply trimmed with the outer leaves taken off. Always served with a bowl of salad cream for dipping into.

**Beetroot:** Pickled from a jar. Baby beetroot are good, but my favourite is crinkle cut.

## THE SPECIAL SALADS

**Coleslaw:** A staple of every Irish salad plate. Shred half a head of white/Dutch cabbage as finely as possible into a large bowl – I use a mandolin. Add a grated carrot and a little salt and black pepper. Bind everything together with a couple of spoonfuls of mayonnaise. Keep chilled until ready to use.

**Egg mayonnaise:** Four hardboiled eggs (see page 11) are cooked, peeled and cut in half lengthways. Each half is then topped with a teaspoon of mayonnaise and a light dusting of paprika.

**Potato salad:** A great way to use up leftover potatoes. Dice cooked potatoes into small cubes and put them in a large bowl. Add two finely chopped scallions, a small handful of chopped fresh parsley and a little salt and pepper. Bind together with a few spoonfuls of mayonnaise and 1 tablespoon of salad cream. Keep chilled until ready to serve.

## THE EXTRAS

**New potatoes:** A bowl of new-season Irish potatoes and butter would always be served with our salad plate.

**Bread and butter:** This could be homemade brown bread, some white sliced pan or a crusty bread roll – it doesn't matter as long as there is plenty of butter on it.

**Cheese:** Triangle slices of red Cheddar.

# A modern salad plate

It will come as no surprise that there are lots of North African, Middle Eastern and Persian influences on my modern take on a salad plate, or in this case, a salad buffet. With a selection of flavours, textures and temperatures, there is something here for everyone. Serve all of these or just a few with the hummus kawarma (page 112) or maybe a roast chicken (page 134) that has been seasoned with lots of ras el hanout (page 14) and stuffed with a quartered lemon, or maybe a whole roast cauliflower (page 138) and lots of flatbread (page 11) to mop up the salads. In an ideal world this is one of those meals that would last for hours on a warm summer evening surrounded by friends or family sharing not only food, but conversations, memories and togetherness.

All salads serve 4

## Roast carrot, cumin & blood orange salad

450g carrots, peeled and cut into quarters lengthways

2 tbsp olive oil

1 tsp cumin seeds

½ tsp paprika

salt and freshly ground black pepper

2 blood oranges, peeled and segmented

2 tbsp good-quality extra-virgin olive oil

1 small bunch of fresh flat-leaf parsley, roughly chopped

Preheat the oven to 180°C fan. Line a large baking tray with non-stick baking paper.

Put the carrots in a large bowl with the regular olive oil, cumin and paprika. Season with salt and pepper and give everything a good mix to coat the carrots. Spread the carrots out on the lined tray and roast in the preheated oven for 25–30 minutes, until they are cooked and slightly charred.

Allow to cool completely before arranging on a serving platter. Dress with the orange segments, drizzle over the extra-virgin olive oil and garnish with a sprinkling of parsley.

## Warm feta & green olive salad

200g feta cheese

200g green olives

4 garlic cloves, thinly sliced

3 strips of lemon rind

1 sprig of fresh rosemary

100ml good-quality olive oil

fresh bread, to serve

Preheat the oven to 160°C fan.

Crumble the feta into a small baking dish.

Using the palms of your hands, squash the olives and put them in a saucepan along with the garlic, lemon rind and rosemary. Pour in the olive oil and put the pan on a medium heat. Once everything starts to sizzle in the oil, take the pan off the heat and carefully pour everything over the feta. Bake in the preheated oven for 10 minutes.

Serve immediately with lots of fresh bread for dipping in the oil. Make sure to have a small bowl on the side for the olive stones.

# Zâalouk

2 large aubergines

4 tbsp olive oil

6 garlic cloves, chopped

1 tbsp tomato purée

2 tsp ground cumin

½ tsp smoked paprika

2 ripe tomatoes,
deseeded and chopped

50ml water

1 small bunch of fresh
flat-leaf parsley, chopped

1 small bunch of fresh
coriander, chopped

2 tbsp tahini

juice of ½ lemon

a squeeze of honey

salt and freshly ground
black pepper

good-quality extra-virgin
olive oil, for drizzling

Preheat the oven to 180°C fan.

Pierce the skin of each aubergine several times with a sharp knife, then put them in a baking dish and drizzle with 2 tablespoons of the oil. Rub the oil into the aubergine skin, then transfer the dish to the oven and cook for 25–30 minutes. When cooked, the aubergines should look like they have collapsed and should feel soft. Allow to cool.

Heat the remaining 2 tablespoons of oil in a saucepan over a medium heat. Add the garlic and cook for 1 minute, then add the tomato purée, cumin and paprika and cook for 1 minute more. Stir in the diced tomatoes and water, reduce the heat slightly and simmer for 5 minutes. Scrape into a large bowl and allow to cool completely.

When the aubergines are cool enough to handle, cut them open and scoop out the flesh with a spoon, leaving the skin behind. Using a sharp knife, roughly chop the aubergine flesh, then add it to the tomatoes along with the parsley, coriander, tahini, lemon juice and honey. Give everything a good mix, then season to taste with salt and pepper or more honey or lemon if required. Transfer to a serving bowl and keep in the fridge until required. Drizzle with extra-virgin olive oil before serving.

# Cucumber & mint salad

2 cucumbers, peeled
and thinly sliced

1 small bunch of fresh
mint, leaves picked
and finely shredded

juice of ½ lemon

4 tbsp olive oil

salt and freshly
ground black pepper

Put the cucumber slices, mint, lemon juice and oil in a large bowl and gently toss together. Season with salt and pepper and transfer to a serving bowl. Refrigerate for at least 30 minutes before serving to let the flavours marry together.

# Roast beetroot, garlic & walnut labneh

2 medium-sized
beetroot, scrubbed

1 whole garlic bulb

2 tbsp olive oil

salt and freshly ground
black pepper

60g walnuts

500g labneh (page 13)

good-quality extra-
virgin olive oil, for
drizzling

Preheat the oven to 180°C fan.

Put a large sheet of foil on the countertop. Put the beetroot and the
whole garlic bulb in the middle of the foil. Drizzle the beetroot and
garlic with the olive oil and rub it into each one, then season with salt
and pepper. Wrap them up in the foil and put on a baking sheet, then
roast them in the oven for 1¼ hours, until cooked – the tip of a sharp
knife should easily pierce the beetroot.

Put the walnuts on a small baking tray and add to the oven for the
final 15 minutes of the cooking time. Remove both the walnuts and
the foil parcel from the oven. Carefully open the foil parcel – watch
out for escaping steam – and allow to cool completely.

I recommend you use clean rubber gloves for the next stage, as it
will stop your hands from turning purple! When the beetroot are cool
enough to handle, peel them. Using a box grater, grate the beetroot
on the side with the biggest teeth. Put the grated beetroot on a plate
and set aside.

Squeeze the garlic cloves out of the bulb onto a chopping board and
chop finely. Roughly chop the toasted walnuts.

Put the labneh in large bowl along with the roasted garlic, season
with salt and pepper and beat together. Fold in the grated beetroot
and most of the walnuts. Transfer to a serving dish and chill for half
an hour before serving to let the flavours marry together.

Garnish with the reserved walnuts and a drizzle of extra-virgin olive
oil before serving.

# Homemade beans on toast

I know you could simply open a tin of baked beans and have a meal ready in a matter of minutes – and I do that myself sometimes, as you'll see in the variations on the next two pages – but I also love taking the time to prepare a homemade version of this much-loved classic. A warming and hearty meal packed full of flavour, there is just something about the smoky taste that is so evocative. It makes me think of having beans on toast made over an open fire on camping trips as a child.

Serves 4

25g butter

1 tbsp vegetable oil

1 onion, finely chopped

125g smoked bacon lardons (or omit the bacon and add 1 tsp smoked paprika instead if you want to keep this vegetarian)

1 red or yellow pepper, thinly sliced

2 tbsp tomato purée

2 x 400g tins of cannellini beans, drained and rinsed

100ml vegetable stock

2 shots of espresso or ½ cup strong black coffee

2 tbsp balsamic vinegar

2 tbsp black treacle

salt and freshly ground black pepper

1 small bunch of fresh parsley, finely chopped

**To serve:**

hot buttered toast

Heat the butter and oil in a frying pan over a medium heat. When the butter has melted and is starting to foam, add the onion and gently cook for about 5 minutes, stirring occasionally. Turn up the heat a little, add the bacon and pepper and cook for another 5 minutes, again stirring occasionally. Add the tomato purée and cook for 1 minute, stirring regularly.

Add the beans, stock, espresso, vinegar and treacle and season with salt and pepper. Give everything a good mix and bring to a boil, then reduce to a simmer for 15–20 minutes, until the sauce has thickened.

Stir in the parsley and serve on top of hot buttered toast, with extra toast for dipping.

# Variations

## PIMP YOUR BEANS

Years ago I was watching something on television hosted by Gordon Ramsey and he was heating up a tin of beans, but he added a knob of butter and a squeeze of tomato ketchup to them. Out of curiosity, the next time I was heating up a tin of beans, I tried it – and my mind was blown. I don't think I've had plain baked beans ever since.

**SIMPLE BAKED BEANS**
Add 25g butter and 25g tomato ketchup to a tin of beans and warm through.

### SMOKED BACON & COFFEE BEANS

This is a much quicker version of the recipe on page 164. Fry some smoked bacon lardons in a pan until crisp, then add a tin of beans and ½ teaspoon of instant coffee. Give everything a good stir as it heats to dissolve the coffee granules.

### SPICY BEANS

Fry one finely chopped onion in a little butter. After a few minutes, add two cloves of chopped garlic and one finely chopped fresh red chilli. Fry for another minute before adding the tin of beans, then stir and heat through.

### SAUSAGES & BEANS

Cook some cocktail sausages in a frying pan. When they are cooked through, add a pinch of dried sage and a tin of beans, then stir and heat through.

# Coconut & red lentil dal

The more I write about food, the more one thing in particular has become clear to me. No matter where you are in the world, we all love food that gives us nourishment, comfort and familiarity. In Ireland it's probably a potato dish, while in Morocco it's couscous and in India it's dal. I love dal, especially a coconut dal. Served with freshly cooked basmati rice and naan or flatbreads, it makes a beautiful meal. If you are making your own flatbreads to serve with this dal, I suggest adding some desiccated coconut, flaked almonds and sultanas to give you the flavours of a Peshwari naan.

Serves 4

350g dried red lentils

1 small bunch of fresh coriander

2–3 tbsp vegetable oil

2 onions, finely chopped

6 garlic cloves, finely chopped

a thumb-sized piece of fresh ginger, peeled and finely chopped

1 tsp mustard seeds

1 tsp cumin seeds

1 tsp ground coriander

1 tsp ground turmeric

1 tbsp tomato purée

900ml vegetable stock

1 x 400g tin of coconut milk

1 fresh red chilli, left whole

salt and freshly ground black pepper

Put the lentils in a fine mesh sieve and rinse them under cold running water to remove any dust. Pick the coriander leaves from the stalks. Keep the leaves for garnish and finely chop the stalks.

Heat 2 tablespoons of the oil in a large heavy-based pan over a low heat. Add the onions and cook for 10 minutes, stirring occasionally, until they start to turn brown. Add the garlic and ginger and cook for 2 minutes, adding another tablespoon of oil if it's looking dry. Add all the spices and the chopped coriander stalks and cook for 1 minute, then stir in the tomato purée and cook for 1 minute more.

Stir in the rinsed lentils along with the stock and coconut milk. Pierce the whole chilli a few times with the tip of a sharp knife, then nestle it into the lentils. Bring to a boil, then reduce to a simmer and cook for about 30 minutes, until the lentils are tender. Season well with salt and pepper and stir in half of the coriander leaves.

Divide the dal among warm bowls with some basmati rice and garnish with the remaining coriander leaves, some slices of red chilli and thin matchsticks of fresh ginger. Serve with lime wedges on the side for squeezing over and warm naan or flatbreads to clean the bowl.

**To garnish:**

1 fresh red chilli, thinly sliced into rings

a thumb-sized piece of fresh ginger, peeled and cut into matchsticks

**To serve:**

steamed basmati rice

1 lime, cut into wedges

warm naan or flatbreads (page 11)

# Pineapple or egg?

Life is full of important decisions. Thankfully, they are not all as hard as the ones in this recipe: skin on or off? Frying pan or griddle pan? Pineapple or egg?

There are no wrong answers here – your gammon will be beautiful whatever way you choose to cook it. It doesn't matter whether or not you like crispy skin or char lines. Most importantly, it doesn't matter if you prefer sweet, caramelised pineapple or a soft fried egg. Just don't try both at the same time, as I once did – it simply doesn't work.

Whichever way you're having it, please source the best gammon steak you can. Lots of independent butchers out there are stocking free-range bacon, and as with all meat, if you can afford to spend that little bit more, you won't be disappointed.

Serves 2

2 gammon steaks

2 tbsp vegetable oil

salt and freshly ground black pepper

2 tinned pineapple rings or 2 free-range eggs

a pinch of light brown sugar (if using the pineapple)

If your gammon still has the skin attached, you have two options:

**1.** Trim off the skin and some of the excess fat.

**OR**

**2.** Use scissors to snip the skin at 2cm intervals. This will stop the gammon curling when it's being cooked.

To cook it, you again have two options:

**1.** Heat the oil in a large frying pan over a medium heat. Season the gammon with a little salt and some black pepper. Put the gammon in the pan and cook for 5 minutes, until golden brown. Turn over and cook for another 5 minutes, until the gammon is cooked through. If it isn't, give it another minute on each side.

**OR**

**2.** Heat a grill pan over a medium-high heat. Rub a little oil onto each gammon steak and season with a little salt and black pepper. Put the gammon in the pan and cook for 3 minutes. Don't turn the steaks over but rather turn them 90 degrees and cook for another 3 minutes – this will create the criss-cross effect of the griddle lines. Turn over and cook for a further 4–5 minutes, until cooked through. ⊙

Finally, your last two options – pineapple or egg:

**1.** If you want pineapple, turn your grill to the highest setting. Put the two pineapple slices on a baking tray lined with foil. Sprinkle a little light brown sugar on top of the pineapple, then put the tray under the grill for 2–3 minutes to caramelise the pineapple.

OR

**2**. If you want a fried egg, crack your egg onto a saucer. Heat 1 tablespoon of butter or oil in a frying pan over a medium-low heat. Gently slide the egg into the pan, reduce the heat to low, season with salt and pepper and cover the pan with a lid, then cook for 3 minutes. Make sure the white is set before serving – if not, just cook it a little longer. I like to cook my eggs sunny-side-up (see page 11) to serve with gammon.

To serve, put the gammon steaks on two warmed plates and top with either the pineapple or egg. I like to serve chips and some green veg with the pineapple version or mash and beans with the egg option.

# Steak frites

A classic French dish, with Irish ingredients, written in English – how European! We have some of the best food products, farmers and food producers here in Ireland and I will champion our food, especially our dairy, beef and salt, forever. I aways make my garlic butter with the best butter in the world – Irish butter – while the steak is seasoned with the best salt in the world, from Achill or Dingle.

Serves 2

2 x 220g steaks (sirloin or rib-eye are my preferred cuts)

4 large potatoes, ideally a combination of waxy and floury, such as King Edwards and Maris Pipers

vegetable oil, for deep-frying

salt and freshly ground black pepper

**To serve:**

a pinch of flaky sea salt

garlic butter (page 12)

Take your steaks out of the fridge about 30 minutes before you start to cook. They will be so much more tender if you cook them from room temperature.

Peel the potatoes and cut them into whatever size chips you prefer. Put the batons in a large bowl of cold water and leave for half an hour. (If you would prefer to make oven chips, see the spice bag recipe on page 180.)

Preheat the oil in your deep-fryer to 140°C.

Drain the potatoes and put them in a clean tea towel to dry. Working in batches, put the chips in the basket of the deep-fryer and lower it into the hot oil. Fry for about 8 minutes, until the chips are cooked but not coloured. Tip the chips out onto a plate, then turn the fryer up to 180°C.

Put a frying pan big enough for the two steaks on a high heat without any oil and heat the pan until it's smoking hot. Season the steaks on a board or plate by lightly rubbing them with a little oil, a light sprinkling of salt and lots of freshly ground black pepper.

How you cook your steaks depends on the cut and how thick they are, but as a general rule, cook for 2 minutes on each side for rare, 3 minutes for medium, 4 minutes for medium-well and 5 minutes for well done. However, remember that the thinner the steak is, the less time it will take to cook. Now for an important step: let the steaks rest on a warm plate in a warm place for a few minutes while you finish the chips. Resting the meat allows it to become more tender, as the meat can relax and the juices can redistribute.

Finish cooking the chips by frying them in the hotter oil in batches for 3–4 minutes, until crisp and golden brown. Drain on kitchen paper and season with flaky sea salt.

Serve the steaks with a pinch of flaky sea salt and a slice of garlic butter on top to let it melt in, with the chips on the side.

# Lasagne, coleslaw & chips

In the inaugural issue of *Scoop* magazine, my friend Marcus O'Laoire described lasagne, coleslaw and chips as an Irish holy trinity of food and I completely agree. I really don't think we could have made this Italian classic any more Irish than by turning it into a double carb hit with a side of cabbage. I have made so many lasagnes over the years – first when helping Mum when she had her catering business and then in my work as a chef – that truth be told, I went off it for a long time. But my love for this combination is well and truly back.

Serves 4

**For the beef ragù:**

2 tbsp vegetable oil

1 medium onion, finely diced

125g bacon lardons

4 garlic cloves, finely chopped

500g beef mince

2 carrots, finely diced

2 celery sticks, finely diced

1 glass of red wine (optional)

2 tbsp tomato purée

1 x 400g tin of chopped tomatoes

2 bay leaves

1 tsp dried oregano

salt and freshly ground black pepper

To make the beef ragù, heat the oil in a large frying pan over a medium heat. Add the onion and cook for 8 minutes, stirring occasionally, until softened, then add the bacon lardons and cook for another 5 minutes. Add the garlic and cook for 2 minutes more.

Turn up the heat and add the beef mince. Break it up with a spoon but don't overmix or break it up too much – try to keep some texture. Allow it to get some colour before stirring it to brown all over. This will take 8–10 minutes.

Add the carrots and celery and cook for 2 minutes, then pour in the red wine (if using) and let it evaporate completely. Add the tomato purée and cook for another 2 minutes.

Stir in the tin of chopped tomatoes, then half-fill the tin with water, swirl it around to catch all the remaining tomato stuck to the sides and add it to the pan. Add the bay leaves and oregano and season with salt and pepper. Bring to a boil, then reduce the heat and simmer gently for 45 minutes, adding a dash of water if it starts to look too dry.

While the ragù simmers, you can make the cheese sauce as per the recipe on page 10.

Preheat the oven to 180°C fan. Grease a 20cm square baking dish. ➔

1½ batches of béchamel cheese sauce (page 10)

6–9 dried lasagne sheets

75g grated cheese (I like to use a mix of Cheddar and mozzarella)

**To serve:**

shop-bought coleslaw

chips (page 180 or shop-bought)

Put one-quarter of the cheese sauce on the bottom of the prepared dish and spread it out. Put two or three lasagne sheets on top of the sauce. Top the pasta with half of the beef ragù, then one-quarter of the cheese sauce and another layer of pasta sheets. Top with the rest of the ragù, one-quarter of the cheese sauce and the rest of the pasta sheets. Finally, top with the rest of the cheese sauce and scatter the grated cheese over the top.

Transfer to the preheated oven and cook for 40–45 minutes, until the top is golden brown and the lasagne is cooked through and bubbling.

Remove from the oven and allow to stand for about 10 minutes before cutting into slices. Serve with coleslaw and chips on the side.

# Fish lasagne
## with garlic bread topping

If lasagne, chips and coleslaw is the Irish holy trinity, then lasagne and garlic bread is a match made in heaven. Taking inspiration from a fish pie and marrying it with a lasagne, this crunchy garlic bread-topped fish lasagne is surprisingly simple to make.

Serves 4

**For the velouté sauce:**

75g butter

50g plain flour

600ml fish stock

1 onion, thinly sliced

2 garlic cloves, finely chopped

200g baby spinach

1 x 250g tub of mascarpone cheese

600g mixed fish – I use a mix of salmon, haddock, smoked cod and prawns

zest of ¼ lemon

freshly ground black pepper

**To assemble the lasagne:**

6–9 dried lasagne sheets

1 shop-bought garlic bread (the baguette kind works best)

1 ball of fresh mozzarella, cut into small cubes

Start by making the velouté sauce. Melt 50g of the butter over a medium heat in a medium-sized heavy-based saucepan. When it's starting to foam, add the flour and cook for 1 minute to make a roux. Pour in one-quarter of the stock and whisk for 2 minutes, then whisk in the rest of the stock and simmer for 5–8 minutes, whisking occasionally, until nicely thickened. Remove the pan from the heat and allow to cool.

Melt the remaining 25g of butter in a large frying pan over a medium heat. When it's starting to foam, add the onion and cook for 8–10 minutes, stirring occasionally, until softened. Add the garlic and cook for 2 minutes before adding the spinach and allowing it to wilt. Remove the pan from the heat and allow to cool.

Preheat the oven to 180°C fan. Grease a 20cm square baking dish.

Whisk the mascarpone into the cooled sauce. Pour two-thirds of the sauce into a large bowl and gently fold in the onion and spinach mixture along with the fish, lemon zest and some black pepper.

Pour half of the reserved plain sauce into the bottom of the prepared dish and spread it out. Put two or three lasagne sheets on top of the sauce. Top the pasta with half of the fish mixture, another layer of pasta sheets, the rest of the fish mixture and a final layer of pasta sheets. Spread the rest of the plain sauce on top of the lasagne.

Cut the garlic bread into small cubes and dot them across the top of the lasagne, followed by the mozzarella cubes nestled into the garlic bread.

Transfer to the preheated oven and cook for 40–45 minutes, until the top is golden brown and the lasagne is cooked through and bubbling.

Remove from the oven and allow to stand for about 10 minutes before cutting into slices to serve.

# Spice bag

Confession time: I had my first spice bag while I was writing this book. I had spent a day writing and just wasn't in the mood for cooking, so when Daithí suggested a takeaway, I jumped at the idea. When he asked me what I wanted, the words 'spice bag' just flew out. I'd never had one – or even had the desire to have one – but I suddenly found myself ordering one. Maybe it's because I had been thinking so much that day about what traditional Irish cooking is and was trying to think of our modern dishes that are distinctly Irish, in much the same way as I see a jambon being a traditional Irish bake. Anyway, from the moment I opened the bag and the spicy steam escaped to eating the last chip coated in its spices, I was hooked. Why had I waited so long?

For those of you who don't know what a spice bag is, I think it's the newest traditional Irish dish in the same way that lasagne, coleslaw and chips can be thought of as uniquely and traditionally Irish. First sold by the Sunflower Chinese takeaway in Templeogue, Dublin in 2010, a spice bag contains chips, crispy chicken, peppers, onions, chilli and a mix of spices, all tossed together and served in a bag. When you first (or in my case, finally) taste one, you will understand why it has such a cult following.

Serves 2

3 large potatoes, peeled (about 750g peeled weight) – Roosters work well for this

vegetable oil

1 medium onion, thinly sliced

1 red pepper, thinly sliced

50g plain flour

1 egg, beaten

80g fresh white breadcrumbs

2 chicken fillets, each one cut into 6 strips

1 fresh red chilli, thinly sliced

3 scallions, thinly sliced at an angle

Preheat the oven to 200°C fan. Line a large baking sheet with non-stick baking paper.

Mix all the spice bag seasoning ingredients together in a small bowl.

Cut the potatoes into chips and pat them dry with a clean tea towel. Put the chips in a large bowl with 1 tablespoon of oil and a generous teaspoon of the seasoning and toss to coat. Spread the chips out in a single layer on the lined baking sheet and cook in the preheated oven for 35 minutes, turning once during the cooking time.

Put the onion and pepper in the same bowl that you used for the potatoes with 1 tablespoon of oil and another teaspoon of the seasoning. Toss to coat and set aside.

While the chips are cooking, prepare the chicken. Put the flour and 1 teaspoon of the seasoning in a wide, shallow bowl and mix to combine. Put the beaten egg and breadcrumbs in two separate wide, shallow dishes, ➔

**For the spice bag seasoning:**

2 tbsp flaky sea salt

1 tsp Chinese five-spice powder

1 tsp ground white pepper

½ tsp dried chilli flakes

Working with one strip of chicken at a time, dip it first in the seasoned flour, followed by the egg and finally the breadcrumbs, making sure the chicken is completely covered each time. Put the breaded chicken on a plate while you work on the rest. And here's a little tip: keep one hand wet and the other hand dry, so in other words, use one hand to pick up the chicken and take it out of the egg, then use the other hand to remove it from the flour and breadcrumbs.

After 35 minutes, take the chips out of the oven. Gently turn the chips over and scatter the onion and pepper over them. Return to the oven to cook for a further 15 minutes.

Heat some vegetable oil in high-sided frying pan over a medium heat. Working in batches so that you don't overcrowd the pan, shallow-fry the chicken strips until they are golden brown all over and cooked through, keeping the cooked ones warm in the oven as you go. (See page 17 for tips on shallow-frying.)

Remove the chips and vegetables from the oven and transfer them to a large, clean bowl. Add the fried chicken strips, chilli, scallions and 1 teaspoon of the seasoning and toss to combine and coat everything in the spice.

If you can get your hands on chip shop bags, put everything in that for an authentic serve. If not, warm bowls will do. Serve with dips of your choice: I like Kewpie mayo and sweet chilli sauce with mine.

# Old (Bay) bag

How do you modernise something (a spice bag) that we think of as traditional yet is only a few years old? By blending it with a classic combination of flavours that is as Irish as they come: seafood and black pudding. Traditional, classic, modern and contemporary, it's the ultimate bag of flavour. Do try to get your hands on proper Old Bay seasoning, but if it's not available, check out my version on page 13 for an alternative.

Serves 2

3 large potatoes, peeled (about 750g peeled weight) – Roosters work well

3 tbsp vegetable oil

4 tsp Old Bay seasoning

130g black pudding, cut into bite-sized pieces

1 medium onion, thinly sliced

1 yellow pepper, thinly sliced

50g garlic butter (page 12)

200g raw prawns

1 lemon, cut into wedges

a small handful of fresh curly parsley, finely chopped

a small handful of fresh chives, finely chopped

Preheat the oven to 200°C fan. Line a large baking sheet with non-stick baking paper.

Cut the potatoes into chips and pat them dry with a clean tea towel. Put the chips in a large bowl with 1 tablespoon of the oil and a generous teaspoon of the Old Bay seasoning and toss to coat. Spread the chips out in a single layer on the lined baking sheet and cook in the preheated oven for 35 minutes, turning once during the cooking time.

Put the black pudding, onion and pepper in the same bowl that you used for the potatoes along with 1 tablespoon of the oil and another teaspoon of Old Bay. Toss to coat and set aside.

After 35 minutes, take the chips out of the oven. Gently turn the chips over and scatter the onion, pepper and black pudding over them. Return to the oven to cook for a further 15 minutes.

Heat the remaining tablespoon of oil and the garlic butter in a large frying pan over a medium heat. Once the butter has melted and is starting to foam, turn up the heat and add the prawns and the final 2 teaspoons of Old Bay. Cook for 6–8 minutes, tossing the prawns in the butter every minute or so, until they have turned pink and are cooked through. Season the prawns with the juice from one lemon wedge and scatter over the parsley and chives.

Remove the chips, vegetables and black pudding from the oven. If your pan that you cooked the prawns in is big enough, put everything into the pan and toss together to coat in all that glorious garlic butter. If not, simply divide the chips, veg and black pudding between two warm bowls and divide the prawns and garlic butter over the top. Serve with the remaining lemon wedges.

# Supper

# Hot milk & honey

To me, one of the most comforting things in life is a mug of warm milk and honey. Growing up on Duke Street in Athy there was no central heating and the house was quite cold during the winter, but Mum made sure we were warm going to bed. We got hot water bottles, cosy 1980s versions of the now-popular onesies and a warm drink in our own personalised mugs. My favourite was always hot milk and honey, which seemed to magically keep me warm from the inside throughout the night.

Serves 1

1 mug of milk

honey to taste (I like to use 1 large tsp)

a pinch of ground cinnamon

I always start by warming my mug with freshly boiled water from the kettle.

Heat the milk in a small saucepan, being careful not to allow it to boil. Pour the water out of the mug and give it a quick dry, then pour in the milk, stir in honey to taste and sprinkle a pinch of ground cinnamon on top.

## Note

The mug in the photo is my original childhood mug and is over 40 years old.

# Masala chai

For years I would have called this chai tea, but after a recent online course with Mallika Basu about food, culture and mindset, I realised that I had effectively been saying 'tea tea'. You see, the word 'masala' means 'spice' and the word 'chai' means 'tea'. We all make mistakes when we are learning, so don't be worried if you make a mistake too when it comes to learning about new cuisines, trying new foods or even pronouncing new words. I believe that one of the greatest gifts we've been given as a nation is that other people want to come to Ireland and make it their home, both out of choice and out of necessity, bringing a world of influence and flavour with them. We can all learn from them, and most importantly, enjoy the connection and experiences we can share over the one thing we all have in common: food.

Serves 2

6 green cardamon pods

4 black peppercorns

2 cloves

½ cinnamon stick

2 mugs of milk

2 tsp loose black tea leaves, such as Assam

2 slices of fresh ginger

a pinch of ground nutmeg or a grating of fresh nutmeg

2 tsp sugar or honey (optional)

Put the cardamon, peppercorns, cloves and cinnamon stick in a pestle and mortar and crush together but keep them quite coarse.

Put the crushed spices in a small saucepan with the milk, loose tea leaves, ginger and nutmeg. Bring to a boil, then reduce the heat and simmer for 10 minutes, stirring regularly to make sure the milk doesn't stick to the bottom of the saucepan.

Strain the tea into two warm mugs and stir in the sugar or honey if you want to sweeten it.

# Cereal & warm milk

I've already talked about the nostalgia of having hot milk at bedtime as a kid on page 188, but to be honest, hot milk was even better when it was poured over cereal, my personal favourite being hot milk and cornflakes.

I realise that this chapter is full of quite simple, humble recipes and ideas, which some people might think are frivolous or not worthy of being included as recipes in a cookbook at all. But as I wrote this book, I realised that this is what Irish cooking is: simple, humble, honest food that fills you with warmth, is packed with flavour and nourishes you from within. When I started writing down ideas for this book, many were based on my childhood memories – and yes, hot milk and cereal was a favourite – but the more I thought about it, the clearer it became to me that my parents didn't just give me hot milk and cereal to fill me up. They gave it to me to protect me and keep me warm during cold times. In this book, I'm not just writing about Irish cooking; I'm writing about the Irish way of life, the Irish way of coping, the Irish way of being, the Irish way of surviving and the Irish way of protecting those we love with whatever we have available.

Serves 1

**enough milk to fill your favourite bowl**

**a bowl of your favourite cereal**

Heat the milk in a saucepan over a medium heat, making sure it doesn't boil. Pour the hot milk over the cereal and enjoy. For me, eating this now is a brief escape from reality and gives me a sense of calmness and reassurance – hands warm from the bowl, nose filled with the soothing scent of warm milk and the cereal, belly full and content.

# Cherry & dark chocolate flapjack

Sometimes you just need chocolate in the evening, that sweet hit that can't be replaced by anything else. This chewy, chocolatey traybake includes the beautiful flavour of Amarena cherries and a subtle hint of cinnamon. It's one of those treats where a little goes a long way, so cut it into bite-sized squares and have one or two for the perfect night-time treat.

Makes 1 x 20cm square tray

175g butter

100g light brown sugar

60g golden syrup

300g porridge oats

100g Amarena cherries, cut into quarters

75g dark chocolate chips

½ tsp ground cinnamon

1 tsp vanilla bean paste

Preheat the oven to 180°C fan. Line a 20cm square baking tin with non-stick baking paper.

Melt the butter, brown sugar and golden syrup in a saucepan over a medium heat, then remove the pan from the heat and allow to cool. It needs to be cool enough that it won't melt the chocolate.

In a large bowl, mix together the oats, cherries, chocolate chips and cinnamon. Stir the vanilla into the cooled butter mixture before adding it to the oats, giving everything a good mix until well combined.

Transfer to the lined baking tin and level out the top while gently pressing down with the back of a spoon. Bake in the preheated oven for 20–25 minutes, until the oats are turning slightly caramelised at the edges.

Allow to cool completely in the tin before cutting into squares.

# Cheese & crackers

I love cheese and I *really* love Irish cheese. How I eat cheese depends on the day of the week. Early in the week I like a simple sea salt cracker with a thick slice of cheese and maybe a slice of fresh apple. At the weekend I like something a little more indulgent – think hot, gooey cheese with a boozy hit, or cool and creamy with a fruity twist.

I'm not really celebrating a traditional Irish dish here. Instead, I want to celebrate the tradition of Irish cheesemaking, so whatever way you like your cheese, get out and support our amazing Irish cheese producers.

Serves 4

## Weeknight cheese

**Cheese & crackers:** I love a simple sea salt cracker to have with cheese. Preheat the oven to 200°C fan. Put 200g plain four, 1 teaspoon sea salt, 1 teaspoon caster sugar, 2 tablespoons olive oil and about 100ml of water in a large bowl and mix to a rough dough. Sprinkle some plain flour directly onto a sheet of non-stick baking paper, tip the dough out onto it and roll out the dough until it's about 6mm thick. Cut the dough into squares, brush them with a little water and add another sprinkling of sea salt. Prick each square several times with a fork and bake in the preheated oven for 12–15 minutes, until crisp and golden. Allow to cool before you have them with your favourite cheese.

A few hard Irish cheeses I love: Hegarty's (Cork), Templegall (Cork), Mount Leinster (Carlow), Cáis na Tíre (Tipperary) and Mossfield (Offaly)

# Friday night cheese

**Baked cheese with Valentia Island vermouth:** Preheat the oven to 200°C fan. Unwrap a full circle of a Brie or Camembert-style cheese and put it in a baking dish that it fits into snugly. Score a few lines into the top of the cheese with the tip of a sharp knife, sprinkle over 1–2 tablespoons of Valentia Island vermouth and bake in the preheated oven for 15–20 minutes, until the cheese is completely gooey. Serve with crackers for dipping.

A few soft Irish cheeses I love: Cavenbert (Cavan), Wicklow Bán (Wicklow) and Cooleeney (Tipperary)

# Saturday night cheese

**Roast grapes & goat cheese:** This combination of cool, creamy cheese and warm grapes is simply wonderful. Preheat the oven to 180°C fan. Put a bunch of red grapes, still on the stem, in a baking dish, drizzle them with a little olive oil and bake in the preheated oven for 25–30 minutes, until the grapes have softened, are slightly wrinkled and have released some of their juices. Serve with goat cheese that has been topped with a drizzle of honey and some lemon zest and crackers for scooping it all up.

Two Irish goat cheeses I love: St Tola (Clare) and Corleggy Kid (Cavan)

# Instant cheesecake

You're sitting at home and you've had your dinner, but deep down all you want is dessert and you know it's a feeling that will last the night. A plain biscuit won't do; you want a bite of something more indulgent to satisfy that craving that won't go away. Well, here it is: the 1-minute dessert. Even better, you have a few flavours to choose from: raspberry ripple, chocolate and orange, banoffee or PB&J. You're welcome.

## Chocolate & orange

A chocolate digestive topped with a thick layer of cream cheese, a dusting of cocoa powder and a little orange marmalade.

## Raspberry ripple

A digestive biscuit topped with a thick layer of cream cheese and a small spoonful of raspberry jam swirled through the cream cheese.

## Banoffee

A Hobnob biscuit topped with a layer of cream cheese, some sliced banana, a squeeze of caramel sauce and a tiny pinch of instant coffee.

## PB&J

A Hobnob biscuit topped with a layer of peanut butter, followed by a layer of cream cheese, a layer of jam and a couple of salted peanuts.

# Ice cream sandwiches

Ice cream sandwiches were a staple of our summers growing up: a simple slice of vanilla ice cream sandwiched between two Jacob's wafers. I would stand at the kitchen counter while Mum cut the blocks of ice cream. The first sandwich was always Dad's. I would be mesmerised by how thick she'd cut the ice cream for the filling of his sandwich, thinking to myself that one day I'd grow up and make my own that thick!

Makes 2 blocks of ice cream

vegetable oil, for greasing

500ml cream

½ x 400g tin of condensed milk

1 generous tsp vanilla bean paste

shop-bought ice cream wafers

Brush the sides of 2 x 2lb loaf tins with a little vegetable oil and line with cling film, leaving enough cling film hanging over the edges to fold them in on top of the ice cream when you have made it.

Pour the cream, condensed milk and vanilla bean paste into a large mixing bowl. Using an electric hand mixer, whisk until thick and creamy. Divide evenly between the two tins. Use a palette knife to flatten the top and give each tin a good tap on the counter to help any air bubbles escape. Cover with the overhanging cling film and freeze overnight.

To serve, take the ice cream out of the freezer, tip it out of the loaf tins and unwrap it. Put a wafer at the end of the log, cut a slice and add another wafer to the cut edge. How many sandwiches you get depends on how much ice cream is in each one!

# Movie night ice cream

We're not talking plain old vanilla ice cream here – were talking big, bold flavours with lots of texture. These aren't everyday ice creams – they are the type of ice creams you get at the cinema and are meant for cosy nights in front of the telly with a good film.

Daithí and I both love film and for many years have attended both the Dublin International and GAZE film festivals. I particularly love films about food, so please indulge me as I give you recommendations for films to match the flavours.

- For the chocolate and marshmallow, I suggest the Canadian film *Peace by Chocolate*, directed by Jonathan Keijser and based on a true story.

- For the custard cream it has to be something classic and comforting, just like the biscuit, so maybe *Julie & Julia* (my love for Julia Child will never cease).

- For the peanut butter and raspberry, my favourite film of recent years is *The Peanut Butter Falcon*, starring Zack Gottsagen, although it has nothing to do with food!

Serves 6-8

500ml cream

½ x 400g tin of condensed milk

1 generous tsp vanilla bean paste

**Chocolate & marshmallow:**

2 tbsp cocoa powder (add at step 1)

75g chocolate chips (add at step 2)

50g mini marshmallows (add at step 2)

4 Fudge bars, cut into small pieces (add at step 2)

**Step 1:** Pour the cream, condensed milk, vanilla bean paste and whatever step 1 flavours you want to add into a large mixing bowl. Using an electric hand mixer, whisk until thick and creamy.

**Step 2:** Fold in most of the step 2 ingredients. Keep back a little of each to sprinkle over the top at the end.

**Step 3:** Pour into a suitable container or a loaf tin that can be frozen. Use a palette knife to flatten the top and to swirl through any step 3 ingredients. Give the container a good tap on the counter to help any air bubbles escape. Sprinkle over the reserved ingredients from step 2. Cover with a lid or wrap in cling film and put in the freezer to set overnight.

To serve, take the ice cream out of the freezer and let it sit at room temperature for about 20 minutes before scooping into bowls or eating directly from the tub!

**Peanut butter & raspberry:**

2 tbsp peanut butter (add at step 1)

125g fresh raspberries, cut in half (add at step 2)

6 peanut butter cups, cut into pieces (add at step 2)

50g salted peanuts (add at step 2)

2 tbsp raspberry jam (add at step 3)

**Custard cream:**

2 tbsp custard powder (add at step 1)

12 custard creams, cut into small pieces (add at step 2)

1 small pot of pre-made custard (add at step 3)

# Tea & biscuits: Mikado

Over the past few years I've become known for taking iconic biscuits from our childhood and giving them a twist. Think bourbon creams with miso caramel, jammy dodgers with blackcurrant and rosemary, or custard and rhubarb creams. But in this case, I'm sticking with the classic combination of raspberry and coconut, the only difference being the size. You see, when I remember a classic Mikado from my youth, I think about running my finger down the middle to scoop out the jam. Over the years my hands have got bigger and I think the biscuits have got smaller, so it hasn't been possible to recreate that memory – until now! These giant-sized Mikado will give you the opportunity to relive your childhood.

Makes 15

300g raspberry jam

100g desiccated coconut

**For the shortbread:**

220g plain flour, plus extra for dusting

150g butter, diced

70g caster sugar

**For the marshmallow:**

75ml water

6g powdered gelatine

2 egg whites

115g caster sugar

1 tsp vanilla bean paste

pink food colouring

To make the shortbread, put the flour, butter and sugar in a large bowl. Using your fingers, rub everything together until it looks like fine breadcrumbs, then squeeze everything together to form a stiff dough.

Tip the dough out onto a lightly floured surface and roll it out to a thickness of 6mm. Cut the dough into rectangles measuring 9cm x 5cm. Prick each biscuit with a fork three or four times.

Transfer the rectangles to a baking tray lined with non-stick baking paper and chill in the fridge for 15 minutes.

Preheat the oven to 150°C fan.

Bake the shortbread in the preheated oven for 15–20 minutes, until golden brown. Allow to cool on the tray for 5 minutes before using a palette knife to transfer to a wire rack to cool completely.

To make the marshmallow, put 25ml of the water in a small bowl and sprinkle the gelatine powder over the water to allow it to bloom. When blooming gelatine, always add the gelatine to the water (never add the water to the gelatine) to allow it to soften and soak up the water. Set aside. →

Put the egg whites in the bowl of a stand mixer fitted with the balloon whisk attachment.

Put the caster sugar and the remaining 50ml of water in a saucepan. Cook over a medium-high heat until the mixture reaches 124°C on a sugar thermometer. Please be incredibly careful when you work with hot sugar as it can burn badly!

Turn the stand mixer on to its highest speed. While the egg whites are whisking, take the pan with the sugar and water off the heat, then stir the gelatine and the water it was soaked in into the hot sugar. Be careful, as the sugar will bubble and spit.

The egg whites should be light and foamy at this stage. With the mixer still whisking, slowly pour in the warm syrup in a steady stream. Keep whisking until the mixture is smooth and shiny. Add the vanilla and a little pink food colouring. Continue whisking for about 15 minutes, until the mixture is noticeably thicker and cool.

While the marshmallow is whisking, spoon the raspberry jam into a piping bag and fit it with a fine plain nozzzle. Pipe generous lines of raspberry jam down the length of the biscuits. Put a small star nozzle in a clean piping bag and fill it with the marshmallow. Pipe generous lines of marshmallow down either side of the jam.

Working over a bowl with one biscuit at a time, liberally cover the entire biscuit with the coconut, gently shaking off any excess before moving on to the next biscuit.

The Mikado are ready to eat immediately, but in my opinion they are even better the following day. They will keep for five days in an airtight container – if they last that long!

# Tea & biscuits:
## Camomile, lemon & almond

There is something so relaxing about a cup of tea and a biscuit in the evening. I think it's the Irish version of fika, with a little bit of hygge thrown in for good measure. Fika is the Swedish word for a coffee and little snack between meals, something like elevenses or an afternoon treat. Hygge, on the other hand, is a Danish word that's all about a sense of warmth, calmness and comfort. Enjoy these biscuits curled up on the couch with your fluffy socks on and a relaxing cup of camomile tea in your hand for the perfect fika–hygge moment.

Makes 15

180g plain flour

55g caster sugar, plus extra for dusting

125g butter, chilled and diced

40g flaked almonds

1 camomile tea bag, tea removed from the bag

zest of ½ lemon

Put all the ingredients in a large bowl. Using your fingers, rub everything together until it looks like fine breadcrumbs, then squeeze everything together to form a stiff dough.

Tip the dough out onto a lightly floured surface and roll it out to a thickness of 6mm. Use a cookie cutter to stamp out the biscuits. Gather up the dough, roll it out again and repeat until all the dough has been used up.

Transfer the biscuits to a baking tray lined with non-stick baking paper and dust with a little extra caster sugar, then chill in the fridge for 15 minutes.

Preheat the oven to 180°C fan.

Bake in the preheated oven for 15–20 minutes, until golden brown. Allow to cool on the tray for 5 minutes before using a palette knife to transfer to a wire rack to cool completely.

## Note

I make these cookies quite a lot, so I always have a jar of caster sugar and camomile on the go. Simply mix some sugar with some loose, dry camomile and leave to infuse for a few days before using. Sift out what you need for the recipe and top the jar back up with more sugar and extra camomile if required.

# Index

## NINE BEAN ROWS

Nine Bean Rows Books

23 Mountjoy Square

Dublin, D01 E0F8

Ireland

@9beanrowsbooks

ninebeanrowsbooks.com


First published 2024

Text © Graham Herterich, 2024

Photography © Jo Murphy, 2024


ISBN: 978-1-7392105-9-5


Editor: Kristin Jensen

Designer: Jane Matthews janematthews.ie

Food stylist: Orla Neligan cornershopproductions.com

Food photographer: Jo Murphy joanne-murphy.com

Portrait photographers: Elisha Clarke elishaclarke.com (page vi);
Samad Elgarba @samad_elg (page 15)

Shoot assistant: Naomi Dooge naomi-d-food.com

Proofreader: Susan McKeever susanmckeever.biz

Printed by L&C Printing Group, Poland


The paper in this book is produced using pulp from managed forests.

10 9 8 7 6 5 4 3 2 1